IS THE PARTY OVER?

First published by Jacana Media (Pty) Ltd in 2024

10 Orange Street
Sunnyside
Auckland Park 2092
South Africa
+2711 628 3200

www.jacana.co.za

© Oscar van Heerden, 2024

All rights reserved.

ISBN 978-1-4314-3448-0

Cover design by Studio Warburton
Editing by Russell Martin
Proofreading by Lara Jacob
Indexing by Megan Mance
Set in Palatino 10/15pt
Printed and bound by ABC Press
Job no. 004132

See a complete list of Jacana titles at www.jacana.co.za

IS THE PARTY OVER?

Oscar van Heerden

Praise for *Is the Party Over?*

'Perceptive reading of good political books suggests that apart from agency, they are products of curiosity about ideas and the author's ability to gauge the national mood near-accurately, as much as they are about imagination. Striking this balance is difficult for many who write about contemporary events as they battle the temptation to write themselves into the script as heroes who discover and expose villains. That is what Oscar van Heerden has achieved in this book: to offer a balanced account of our national situation with the ruling ANC at the epicentre of political storms.

'Van Heerden, an ANC insider, presents an objective critique of the ANC's ruinous politics of factionalism and infantilisation of governance. Half-eyed suburban readers might read this as an expose or criticism by someone ready to jump ship. Yet, there is a marked difference between criticism and critique. The former is what we read in the opinion pages of newspapers, shebeens and social media. The latter is what we read in this book, offered with a great degree of attention to detail, diligence and turn of phrase that we have come to associate with Van Heerden. I have no doubt that scholars of political science and history will find it hard to exclude this book from their prescribed reading material.'

– Busani Ngcaweni, Senior Research Associate, University of Johannesburg and Adjunct Professor, Wits School of Governance and Soochow University (China)

I dedicate this book to Nadia Goetham, a dear friend whom I miss so very much still. Also, to my wife, Nicky Roberts and my twins, Tessa Andile and Ayanda James.

Contents

Acknowledgements	ix
Author's Note	xi
Prologue: A minute to midnight	1

PART ONE: Nasrec '22

Chapter 1: My journey	7
Chapter 2: A perfect storm	25
Chapter 3: Helter-skelter	41
Chapter 4: Monkey business	57
Chapter 5: Unforced errors and election cock-ups	69
Chapter 6: The accidental chief	83
Chapter 7: Mashatile's back-door presidential gambit	95

PART TWO: Results and Prospects

Chapter 8: Has the ANC fulfilled its mission?	109
Chapter 9: From growth to decline	129
Chapter 10: Quo vadis?	147
Chapter 11: 2024: What prospects?	159
Postscript: The unresolved national question	179
References	189
Notes	183
Index	195

Acknowledgements

I would like to acknowledge and express my gratitude to the SARChi Chair, Prof Chris Landsberg, and the Centre for African Diplomacy and Leadership at the University of Johannesburg. Without their support this book would not have been possible. I also, would like to thank Malcolm Ray for editing the first draft of the book and his continuous advice during its writing. Finally, a huge thank you to Jacana for always having confidence in me. Thank you all.

Author's Note

When I sat down, in the wake of Cyril Ramaphosa's narrow victory over Nkosazana Dlamini-Zuma at the ANC's 54th national conference in December 2017, to write my second book, *Two Minutes to Midnight*, anxieties that had erupted to the surface in the preceding months finally began to spread across the country. It was a strange and perilous turning point in the battle for the party, and the question then was whether Ramaphosa's ANC would survive.

When, in the 2019 elections, Ramaphosa became president of the country, there seemed in that moment to be a collective sigh of relief after a decade of state madness. A celebratory mood enveloped the country; and Ramaphosa's predecessor, Jacob Zuma, seemed covered forever in infamy and oblivion after getting the boot in February 2018.

The mood was fleeting, however. Throughout the first four years of Ramaphosa's presidency, from 2019 to the ANC's 55th national conference at Nasrec in December 2022, there were intense factional struggles within the party and tremendous economic and social events under the onslaught of an unprecedented crisis. No sooner had he ended his first year at the helm than the Covid-19 pandemic struck with such devastating force in early 2020 that the economy seemed to tilt off its axis. By July 2021, raging crowds were running amok in two major provinces of the country, instigated by the pro-Zuma Radical Economic Transformation (RET) faction of the ANC.

But it was another crisis that compelled me to turn my attention to the circumstances of Ramaphosa's first term and their consequences for the ANC. To all appearances, the last two years were not promising. Still reeling from the economic impact of the pandemic, a perfect storm of rolling blackouts, after Eskom had painted itself into an intractable debt corner of R422bn at the time of writing,[1] and rising service delivery failures on the back of a failing state, severely battered the economy. In the tortuous run-up to the conference, the energetic president seemed to retreat into an irascible silence. He had been groping, amid popular frustrations and anger, for a way towards what he called a "Just Energy Transition" and revitalisation of the country's ailing economy. By his own later admission, there was no quick fix.

Then, the summer of 2023 brought another backward step: the bizarre exposé of foreign currency stolen from the president's Phala Phala game farm in the Waterberg by criminals. At first, I wrestled with the saga but then realised that it contained a hidden time bomb set to explode the hope Ramaphosa had kindled in his presidency just as the ANC headed to its conference. I surmised that the timing of the Phala Phala exposé pulsed with the conspiratorial politics that had become the stock in trade of factionalism in the ANC.

WERE MY INSTINCTS UNFOUNDED? In hindsight, Ramaphosa's first term seemed rigged against him. He appeared, as soon as he began his presidency, to be waging a defensive battle against his adversaries inside the ANC and the growing frustrations of citizens who had come to see, perhaps unfairly, the president as the face of a faltering party and state. As we will see in the following chapters, it was the driving force of self-interest and factionalism in the ANC and the chaos of state capture in government that turned the party and state into a tangled mess and consequently bedevilled Ramaphosa's first term.

When I began writing this book, in late January 2023, the question of his survival at the party's 55th conference had been settled by his resounding victory over the RET candidate, Zweli Mkhize. But for a large number of people fed up with loadshedding, corruption and its impact on service delivery, the national conversation had already moved on to the demise of the ANC in the 2024 general elections. A

Author's Note

deluge of scenarios and soothsaying by media commentators and authors predicted the death of the ANC. They were unanimous in declaring that the party was over.

Were these doomsday prophecies correct? In recent years I have publicly and consistently argued that Ramaphosa's survival is inextricably bound up with the fortunes of the ANC at this critical juncture in its history. It is in extending this argument to the 2024 elections that the theme of this book suggested itself to me, not as statement of fact but an inquiry: is the party over? Unlike the prophets of doom, I am convinced that Cyril Ramaphosa's ANC is the best hope for charting the difficult reconstruction and recovery of this country. It is certainly the best hope for redeeming and restoring the rich heritage of the ANC.

However, I am aware, as progressive movements in other developing countries have discovered, that the propensity to singularise the fate of a party, and indeed an entire country, around an individual leader oversimplifies the complex relationship between a diverse party and the stage on which it operates. Symptomatic of these complexities is the question whether one can justifiably speak of a party whose fate orbits around an individual. My view is that influential leaders shape and are shaped by their circumstances. In similar vein, I think that the battle for the ANC is strongly influenced by Ramaphosa as an agent of change, as much as his policy choices are determined by the circumstances in which he and his party operate. It is in this sense that I think Cyril Ramaphosa has a vital role to play in translating the present disorientating context of the ANC and country into a nation-building and national development endeavour.

THIS BOOK STARTS WHERE my previous account of the Ramaphosa presidency left off and relates the beginning of the end of his difficult journey in the ANC and the government he leads. Together with the facts of Ramaphosa's first term, I have had to narrate a period marked by tremendous events: the social and economic ravages of rolling blackouts; falling domestic and foreign investment; collapsing public infrastructure; weak service delivery; spiralling inflation and rising interest rates; and, on the back of all this, rising unemployment and poverty. Each of these difficulties has affected Ramaphosa's fortunes; and with each he has had to stand by his party's glorious history and against its rapid decline into inner-party feuds, corruption and bureaucratic ineptitude.

In narrating this story, I have had to observe the crisis and personality politics inside the party first-hand; for in Ramaphosa's ANC, the ideological debate does not feature as prominently as in Thabo Mbeki's. Ramaphosa is less a theoretician in a National Democratic Revolution than a pragmatic CEO of South Africa Inc. Unlike Mbeki, he is a comrade-turned-businessman-turned president. He is a symbol of moderation and nationhood in a racially fractured and unequal society. As such, he is not preoccupied with the historical and ideological fault lines that fissure society. He is, rather, concerned with the brass tacks of investment and growth which he hopes will resolve the country's problems.

More than in my previous book, in which Ramaphosa began his ascendancy to office promising a "new dawn" against a chaotic backdrop of state capture, I dwell in Part One of this book on his battle in a context of economic decline and swelling anxieties among corporate and individual citizens alike about the future of the ANC and country in what will no doubt go down in history as a seminal moment. That moment is the build-up to the ANC's leadership conference in 2022 and the battle by the RET faction to, once again, win back top positions in the party's powerful National Executive Committee (NEC). At this stage, the fate of Ramaphosa's ANC appears inseparable from the country's declining fortunes: it gives sombre depth to what looks increasingly like the end of the ANC's history. The chapters that make up Part One chronicle, through my first-hand account, the battle for Ramaphosa's ANC at the conference and conclude with his victory over the RET. The section ends, however, with an anti-climax: more plots and subplots that raise questions about the electoral chances of the ANC in 2024.

Against this backdrop, Part Two deals more pointedly with the question: what prospects for the ANC in 2024? Rather than a straightforward narration of the party's electoral decline in recent surveys, I explore the ANC's prospects historically. To understand just how far the party has regressed and how far it has come, it is necessary to track its performance in government against its historical mission. If I can answer that question, then perhaps the party's prospects will become clearer. And here it is important to see that the ANC was shaped by the adjustments it has had to make since 1994 to the shifting social and economic landscape in South Africa. Rather than track those adjustments using electoral milestones, I have periodised key moments that I think have marked significant shifts in the party's leadership and political make-up. Accordingly, I probe more deeply the changing fortunes of the party as it has navigated the vicissitudes of the transition since the end of apartheid.

A note on my political approach and involvement in the ANC

I would like at this point to comment briefly on my own history in the ANC to put my political approach to this book in perspective. Separating party loyalty and critique is never a straightforward task. As a member of the ANC, I am part of the story of a party whose historical mission and vision I have steadfastly shared and helped advance.

However, I do not present an apologia for the departures of the ANC and some of its senior leadership in recent times from the party's founding principles and historical mission. In narrating this story, I have sought to understand the crisis in the ANC not by keeping a critical distance from the party but by immersing myself in the deep well of its politics. The story is told here on the basis of my personal involvement in and observation of the ANC, an organisation to which I have been fortunate to obtain access as a loyal member and active participant in its organisational politics over more than three decades.

I BEGAN LIFE AS AN activist in the ANC at the height of the P.W. Botha government's draconian state of emergency in 1985–6. It was a time of the reawakening of the student movement and organised workers under the umbrella of the United Democratic Front (UDF) after a period of defeat and retreat of the broad liberation movement in the aftermath of the state crackdown on the 1976 student uprisings.

Is the Party Over?

Having grown up in a so-called coloured working-class community on the Cape Flats, I was all too aware of apartheid as an abnormal system in a divided society. But it was during my final year at Harvester Primary in Westridge in Mitchell's Plain that, at the height of the state of emergency, the political consequences of apartheid fired my political consciousness and loyalty to the ANC. In a daily show of force, armed soldiers in Casspirs (what today are known colloquially as Nyalas) and police helicopters would descend on protesting students at schools on the Cape Flats. The upheaval and repression, the teargas and skirmishes between student youth and big, blustering soldiers, were never acceptable to me. As a 13-year-old boy, however, it is not politics but childhood recreation that fires the imagination.

My childhood ended abruptly one morning when I arrived in class to news that one of my classmates, Quintin Bailey, had been shot and killed by apartheid security forces. Bailey was playing in his backyard when he heard skirmishes between students and police and the thud of teargas canisters being fired. When he peered over the fence to see what was going on, a live bullet fired by police ricocheted and killed him. He was 13.

A few days after the tragedy, my entire school marched, silently, in a single file to a church directly opposite the civic centre in Rocklands where the UDF had been launched just two years earlier. There was a tense standoff between heavily armed police and an unarmed group of activists singing "Hamba kahle", a sombre song meaning "goodbye", when we arrived at the burial site. Then all hell broke loose. Police fired teargas. Mourners scattered in all directions. Even primary school students were caught up in the melee. Confused, scared and traumatised, I found my own way home, separated from my classmates and teachers.

When, eventually, I arrived home that evening, I asked my mother why the police had reacted with such brutality to peaceful mourners at a funeral of an innocent victim? Why was Quintin Bailey killed? "Why" is always an existential question. Grappling with it meant coming to terms, for the first time, with apartheid as an existential threat. It was, in hindsight, the beginning, at that tender age, of my political awakening.

Author's Note

THE NEXT TIME I made contact with youth activists was during the first two months of high school in 1986. The state of emergency was still in full swing under the police minister, Adriaan Vlok. So, my induction in liberation politics and activism had taken place at a meeting of activists in a church hall a year previously Through my involvement in a youth group that year, I met student activists who had been visiting high schools in Mitchell's Plain to recruit student leaders and mobilise action against the state of emergency. By the end of 1986, fourteen high schools came to form the Mitchell's Plain Action Committee under the banner of the UDF. A year later, the committee became the Mitchell's Plain Student Congress (MIPSCO). It was during my first year at Portland Senior Secondary that two activists, Gloria Veale and Walleen Mostert, who went on to join the ANC's armed wing, Umkhonto we Sizwe, came to recruit me. The organisation was constituted of two or three representatives per high school. In 1986, I was elected class representative and a year later secretary of the Student Representative Council (SRC). The next year I became president of the SRC, all the while active in MIPSCO and the Cape Youth Congress (CAYCO), which was an after-school youth activity organisation. It was during these formative years that I received my political theory training and my organisational skills and, indeed, sharpened my political activism.

By this time, exactly one year after the state of emergency in 1985–6, I was on the wanted list of the dreaded Security Branch of the South African Police. Through my involvement in student organisations affiliated to regional bodies of student and youth organisations, I was heavily involved in the Western Cape Student Congress (WECSCO). Eventually, in 1989, I became part of the executive committee of the WECSCO as its deputy secretary general. During this volatile period I also got arrested at Cedar Secondary School in Mitchell's Plain together with eleven of my fellow student activists. A stint of "detention without trial" ensued for a brief period after which some of us were transferred to more secure facilities such as Pollsmoor prison in Constantia and Victor Verster prison in Paarl. Others suffered detention without trial and solitary confinement during which time the Special Branch tortured and extracted information from us in less than parliamentary ways. Perhaps if we are to identify a climactic moment of my activism, it was in 1991, soon after the unbanning of liberation organisations, when I was elected to the first National Executive Committee of the Congress of South African Students (COSAS). In retrospect, COSAS's significance lay in its rich history through the 1970s and 1980s when the student movement surged. Its subsequent banning by the apartheid government and unbanning when I got elected seemed to close the circle from resistance to reconstruction.

My loyalty to COSAS, the UDF and the ANC was always governed by my conviction that the banner under which we marched against apartheid was a broad church. Yet, I was never impervious to the contradictions that were bound to emerge once democracy had been achieved, principally economic inequalities and the enormous challenges that followed the negotiated settlement between the old guard in the apartheid government and the ANC. Equally challenging, I knew, were the implications for democracy and social cohesion of the lure of money and power within the post-apartheid state. What I did not imagine was the scale and speed with which the party's control of the state would unleash a new dynamic of factionalism and corruption that eventually not only blurred the distinction between party and state but also divided the party and country ethnically and geographically into competing power blocs and, consequently, ran the entire apparatus of the state and its institutions aground.

And so, the narrative of this book is based even more strongly than my previous work on the circumstances of the ANC's decline during Cyril Ramaphosa's term. We see Ramaphosa trying to revive a long-lost tradition of hope and optimism during the presidency of Nelson Mandela, with this difference: after close on three decades in government, some of the failings of the ANC are now in plain view. Appeals to hope stand on neither the statesmanship and moral pedigree of Mandela, nor the moral high ground of a liberation movement at work to dismantle the institutional and political systems and structures of the apartheid regime. Hope, Ramaphosa is all too aware, is this time a desperate appeal to an otherwise despondent and anxious citizenry fed

Author's Note

up with persistent and growing blunders by his party and government.

All these events have sustained my conviction of the importance of this book. I concluded *Two Minutes to Midnight* with Ramaphosa's rise in an emerging context of inner-party turmoil and economic challenges, portraying him at the beginning of his presidency as a symbol of hope. This book tracks the decline of the ANC at the end of Ramaphosa's first term in the build-up to its 55th conference and the 2024 elections. In relating the general climate and describing the individuals and groups involved in the inner-party struggles, I draw on columns I have written for *Daily Maverick* and News24 over the past five years as well as literature and general reportage on the politics and economics of the country. I have been fortunate in being able to relate the general climate of the ANC's recent elective conference by participating in the conference's resolutions drafting committee, which gave me an inside view of the power dynamics in the build-up to the election of the party's Top 7 leaders.

Oscar van Heerden
March 2023

Prologue
A minute to midnight

In late 2022 a brushfire rumour began spreading through newsrooms and social media platforms across the country. It was not for the first time. There had, since the July riots in 2021, been gossip that Cyril Ramaphosa would throw in the towel and resign his presidency before the end of his first term. Around that time, it was rumoured he had been persuaded by former finance minister Trevor Manuel, who was appointed to lead Ramaphosa's foreign direct investment drive, to stay on.

It was tempting to believe the gossip after Ramaphosa's ascendancy to power. After all, he had, in the wake of his inauguration, entered a public plight so dismal – the social and economic impact of Covid-19 on the country, rampant corruption and raging protests in mid-2021 that, quite literally, set the country ablaze – that his resignation seemed plausible. More plausible, though, was the fact that a successful Ramaphosa presidency lay directly in the path of his adversaries in the pro-Zuma RET faction of the ANC. It seemed that Jacob Zuma's ignominious fall may have emboldened his backers.

Despite the blizzard of stories, many in public preferred to dismiss the rumour as a disingenuous work of fiction spread by Ramaphosa's opponents. Suspicions were immediately directed at the RET. What I discovered is that it mattered less that the rumour wasn't true. What mattered in the public imaginary was the possibility that it might be true. For this and many other reasons, I felt that the truth about Ramaphosa's presidency was all the more interesting for what it revealed about his opponents.

South Africa, by this time, had become a place where power struggles were won and lost not by force of argument, but through subterfuge and conspiracy. There the matter would have rested had it not been for a story related to me by a senior comrade in the ANC that gave the rumour of his resignation a ring of validity.

IT WAS ONE OF THOSE lazy summer days in early January 2023, when the heat hangs over the city of Cape Town like a sweltering hotspot, when my phone rang. I had driven to Cape Town to visit family after a vacation in Knysna with my wife and kids. On the line was the Northern Cape premier, Zamani Saul, whom I regard as a trusted ally and comrade in the Ramaphosa camp. I had come to know Saul in the ANC over a number of years and once spent a great deal of time getting to know him during a party political school we both attended in China in 2018. We also shared a kinship of sorts as public intellectuals. He appreciated my weekly columns and would often phone or WhatsApp me to offer his opinion or criticise some of my arguments.

On that early January afternoon, he wanted to know whether I could meet him on the occasion of the president's January 8 speech. I had no plans to attend the event and had, instead, settled on spending time with my mother until mid-January, when I planned to drive back to Johannesburg. Saul didn't say why he wanted to chat, but if it was urgent, I said to him, I could meet him in Kimberley en route back to Johannesburg.

After a leisurely ten-hour drive from Cape Town, I checked into a lodge in Kimberley, freshened up and, not knowing what to expect at the meeting, dressed in a formal jacket and slacks. Just after lunchtime I drove to see an old friend and comrade at his home on the outskirts of the city. From there I headed to a boutique hotel in the city centre where I was scheduled to meet Saul at 6 pm. From the outside, the hotel looked swanky. The restaurant where I waited was ornately decorated. I had chosen my attire well, I thought.

A few moments later Saul breezed in wearing a T-shirt, shorts, tackies and a broad smile. I was overdressed. No matter, I thought, it would have been marginally embarrassing had I arrived in shorts in a room full of suits. We hugged, sat down and ordered beverages. He seemed energised and excited and wanted my opinion on renewable energy initiatives in the Northern Cape and some game-changing developments in the Port Nolloth harbour.

As I tucked into my food, he began to share his first-hand experience of the president's resignation saga. Cyril Ramaphosa was capable of acts of great tenacity, Saul said to me, but few realised how close he actually came to leaving a week before the party's December conference. I was intrigued but didn't yet know whether our meeting had something to do with party politics. I figured that the purpose of our meeting would soon become clearer.

He spoke almost without pause. Ramaphosa's threat to resign amid the rancour of the Phala Phala saga had been averted when NEC members Gwede Mantashe, Derek Hanekom and several others paid him a visit at the Presidential House in Cape Town one morning in early December and persuaded him to remain in office. That, at least, was what had been reported in the media. "That was not entirely true," Saul said. The president may have agreed in his meeting with Mantashe and Hanekom to stay, he went on to say, but no sooner had they stepped out of the door than Ramaphosa changed his mind. It was Saul that Ramaphosa phoned next: he had decided it was time to go.

The next morning, Ramaphosa cancelled a scheduled press conference where he was expected to publicly announce his decision to stay. The cancellation was broadcast on all television news channels and social media platforms. The chronology fitted Saul's story perfectly. To the public, it was deeply unsettling. A wave of anxiety spread across the country. The rand took a severe beating, tumbling in freefall against the dollar; investors panicked, plunging share prices on the Johannesburg Stock Exchange in a wave of frantic selling. It was a foretaste of things to come. Barely a week before the ANC's all-important national elective conference, the governing party and country seemed adrift.

As I drove back to Johannesburg the next day, it occurred to me that the ANC conference outcome and general fate of the country pivoted on that moment, when Cyril Ramaphosa elected to go. That was not why Saul invited me to meet him, but it is what lingered in my mind in the wake of our meeting.

Part One

Nasrec '22

One

My journey

My involvement in helping to shape the ANC's character as a governing party began in earnest one morning in 1996 with a phone call from a comrade named Spongy Moodley. Moodley was policy coordinator of the ANC's policy and resolutions committee at Luthuli House, whom I had come to know when I was an employee at the party's headquarters from 1996 until 2000. On that day Moodley wanted to know whether I would be interested in joining the committee's technical drafting team.

Suddenly, the course of my life in the ANC, from my student activism during the 1980s and early 1990s to my role in the party as an employee, made perfect sense to me. South Africa was in the throes of the early transition when a host of policy and institutional changes were under way. What better way, I thought, to help shape the policy changes of the ANC as it navigated the policy tensions of the transition than by joining the resolutions committee.

It was around the time that the ANC was preparing for its first elective conference at Mafikeng since winning the 1994 democratic elections, and anxiety was growing within its ranks and the country as a whole about who would eventually succeed Nelson Mandela at the end of his first term. But there was another important battle raging, quietly at first and then in a rowdy conflict between ideological adversaries in the tripartite alliance.

By 1995, THE ANC's economic policy document, the Reconstruction and Development Programme, or RDP, had come under scrutiny by then deputy president Thabo Mbeki and a group of senior officials allied to him in the ANC. Between 1993 and 1995 Mbeki had turned his attention away from the politics of liberation to the business of governing the country and managing the transition to a market economy.

In Mbeki's mind, this path was consistent with the ANC's historical mission. He was, wrote author and journalist Mark Gevisser, "taking the ANC back to its roots".[2] Drawing on the views of Alan Hirsch, who had been the Mbeki presidency's in-house economist, Gevisser wrote that Mbeki's economic policy stance around that time was a reversion in time to the Freedom Charter. In Hirsch's 2005 book, *Season of Hope*, the author draws on a 1956 article in which Nelson Mandela "heralded the charter as a manifesto for, of all things, private enterprise".[3] If Hirsch is correct, then Gevisser argues that the ANC-in-exile's socialism "was a three-decade aberration, a consequence of … the pull of Moscow and the power of the SACP [South African Communist Party]". Mbeki, wrote Gevisser, was merely "shifting things back to the centre".[4]

That meant giving serious attention to foreign direct investment and private sector-friendly economic policies. Mbeki knew all too well that the ANC's 1994 electoral slogan – "a better life for all" – had to be built around investment and growth, not only to deal with the impact of massive illicit financial flows and debt that had been racked up by the apartheid government but, according to Brian Levy, also "to create the possibility of win-win outcomes with shared benefits".[5] As an economic electoral manifesto, the RDP was evidence of this thinking, but as an economic strategy its emphasis on a state-driven redistribution path was wrong-headed.

In 1996, the ANC's embrace of market-friendly policies was manifest. Concerned by the country's debt, the ANC had already, in 1993, signed a letter of intent to the International Monetary Fund

(IMF) committing itself as the future government to a programme of fiscal austerity in return for a loan of $850 million.[6] In his record of the period, Gevisser notes that "at almost exactly the same time, the ANC summarily abandoned the RDP, and Mbeki, who was to be the keynote speaker at its launch, failed to show up".[7] In his absence, wrote Gevisser, the finance minister Trevor Manuel was adamant: "This is not ANC policy," he told the gathering.[8] If Gevisser is right, the RDP's iconic status as an "updated and fleshed-out Freedom Charter" was its shortcoming: "the product of a popular consultative process, it was more the wish list of the 'broad church' that was the ANC than the workable policy of a new government coming into power with the inheritance of crippling debt."[9]

WITHIN THIS CLIMATE of sweeping policy changes and enormous expectations, the fifteen-member drafting team, as it came to be known, convened by the ANC stalwart and NEC member Jeff Radebe, was to play a pivotal role in bringing together all the resolutions and policies of the party and translating them into coherent, workable resolutions for its policy and elective conference. The team's brief meant it carried the technical responsibility in those early years of shifting the ANC-in-exile's socialism, a consequence, as I have pointed out, of the pull of Moscow and the ideological influence of the SACP, back to the centre where it belonged.

The deeply embedded culture and history of exile politics in the ANC's organisational style was expressed by SACP deputy general secretary Jeremy Cronin when he said that "it was common for documents [notably *Strategy and Tactics*] to talk the language of Lenin, which is an attempt to rediscover ANC language of the old, so as to combat the criticism of privatisation, for example, from outside".[10] The irony of Cronin's remark was, of course, lost on him. Against Mbeki's drive to purge the ANC of Leninist language, Cronin was suggesting that the ANC's language was left, but its actions not left enough.

Considering the looming battle at Mafikeng over economic policy, the language of party policy was as important as the content; it was, in Richard Calland's telling, "a reminder that the party remains a party of the left, which is what the debate inside the ANC had been about since the mid-1980s and, to some, for much longer".[11] Thus emerged, in the fierce policy debates leading to Mafikeng, "a clash of culture between the historical, institutional memory of the ANC and the apparatus of governance".[12]

And that's the all-important point, which would have significant implications for the work of the drafting team.

WITH HIS IMPLACABLE intellect and analytical foresight, it was Mbeki who took the lead, along with Kgalema Motlanthe, who was elected ANC secretary general at the 1997 Mafikeng conference, in the debate over modernisation, arguing that the historical rationale for liberation movement policies was outdated. Like Mbeki, Motlanthe was known to have strong views on modernising the party. Though it would take several more years, his assessment of the need for reform was advanced in a paper entitled "Discussion document: The organisational design of the ANC's case for internal renewal; An abridged version".[13] The document, which is thought to have Mbeki's hand in its formulation, is worth quoting in detail:

> The 1994 elections and the final adoption of a new constitution for South Africa in 1996 marked a historic watershed in the struggle for freedom by the ANC ... This new opportunity represented a democratic dispensation involving, among other things, the holding of democratic elections and a democratic parliament, raised the need to re-fashion the ANC's design in order to take full advantage of these new vistas ... This fundamental change in the mission of the ANC, from an extra-parliamentary movement seeking the forceful overthrow of the apartheid regime, to a political party that is part of a normalized political dispensation seeking to rebuild the socio-economic life of South Africa's former oppressed majority, once again implied that the ANC had to design itself to function optimally for the attainment of the new mission ... The most critical weakness of our party constituent structures at all levels is that they do

> not address ... change. Secondly, our structures do not speak to the centres of power of transformation. These two factors constitute the ANC's soft underbelly today ... The first generic recommendation encompasses the ANC leadership organs at all levels; namely that the executives of the ANC at all levels, from branch to province, must be structured in accordance with their responsibility to intervene and provide leadership to all centres of power, viz. the state, civil society, the economy, the battle of ideas, and the continental and global arena.[14]

In truth, the problem did not reside in structures alone. The urgent task, certainly as Mbeki saw it, was to create policy certainty for investors and what he saw as the need to find a bridge between ANC policy and government. "The intergenerational fusion", wrote Gevisser, "and transformation from oppositional identity to government-in-waiting" may have been a triumph for the party at its first above-ground conference in Durban in 1991, but it was hardly a modern political party in government by the time of the policy conference and leadership conference in Mafikeng in 1997.

Thus it was that Mbeki's views in advancing the argument for the modernisation of the ANC, against the wishes of the party's left-wing allies, were articulated in a discussion document written by him for the National General Council, in mid-1997, ahead of the Mafikeng conference. "The state and social transformation" did not bear his name, presumably to pre-empt its outright rejection by the Congress of South African Trade Unions (Cosatu) and the SACP. It was an impressive agenda for modernisation, arguing that the state had to be professionalised,[15] thus raising vexing questions in those initial tentative years of democracy that would be reiterated by Motlanthe in his discussion document a decade later about "future human resource needs in circumstances where party cadres would enjoy a relative degree of economic independence from the organisation and in planning their lives".[16]

Besides the ritual jostling for leadership positions in the party's NEC, the significance of Mafikeng was the challenge, not only of transcending the ANC's status as a liberation movement and becoming a modern political party in those early years, but also of governing through policy rather than ideology and personality. I wholeheartedly shared Mbeki's conviction that unless the ANC started behaving more like a party in government and less like a liberation movement, it would end up fixating on struggle ideologies and organisational practices rather than the practical business of governing the country, steering the economy out of the ruinous debt the apartheid government had left behind, and dealing with the enormous challenges of growth and socio-economic transformation.

WHEN, IN DECEMBER 1997, a thousand delegates gathered in a baking sports hall in Mafikeng, Mbeki took some flak from his left-wing detractors in Cosatu and the SACP who saw the argument for modernisation as a pretext for the ANC's abandonment of the left. Indeed, as Richard Calland has observed, "a 'movement', not a 'party', is how many on the left preferred to see it; a grand coalition that covers the whole of the centre and centre-left ground of South African politics, in partnership with its two great alliance partners Cosatu and the SACP".[17]

With the succession and organisational debate settled, the economic policy debate would come to a head as the primal wound in the relationship between what then appeared to be two factions in the tripartite alliance – one centred around Mbeki's neoliberal agenda and the other around the Cosatu–SACP axis's RDP agenda. And the drafting committee was right in the middle of it. Little did we know then that the standoff over the Growth, Employment and Redistribution (GEAR) strategy would cleave the party into rival factions that would eventually be Mbeki's undoing. But during the build-up to the 1997 policy conference and Mafikeng, the ANC's labour allies were muted in their reaction to GEAR. Mbeki was the steely pragmatist and resolute architect of what Gevisser has described as a period of "necessary pain".[18] And here I want to suggest that although the alliance was divided over ideology, it was not the ethnocentric, clannish factionalism that resulted in Mbeki's early removal from the party in 2007, and then tore the party and country apart during the Zuma years.

In fact, the ideological battle-lines of factionalism, Jeremy Cronin has recalled, began as late as 1990. When the government of F.W. de Klerk unbanned all liberation organisations, Mbeki and those around him "had discussed the relationship between the ANC and SACP among themselves as a faction. They decided that they were going to leave the SACP" and "resigned quietly" in 1990.[19] The division, observes Cronin, was a consequence of the "sharp rivalry" in exile between the Chris Hani and Joe Slovo grouping, on one side, and another grouping that orbited around Thabo Mbeki.[20] It was said at the time that these disagreements centred around whether the SACP membership should remain secret (as it had been since the 1950s) or whether it was time for the SACP to openly embrace mass membership.

By the time of Mafikeng, Mbeki had both intellectually and in policy transcended earlier ideological battles over the terms of the democratic settlement, to focus on more pressing worries of the day. The party was now in office but not quite in power. The economy was still in the hands of a white elite and bleeding in the face of expectations that the terms of the 1994 settlement with the National Party meant deliverance and not betrayal. And yet the ANC's fulminating alliance partners – their vigorous ideological rivalry – seemed to be far too concerned with their own parochial worries to see the big picture. Mbeki wanted to keep the party's attention squarely on the business of governing the country. And despite the mutual antipathy that developed between the two sides, he was open to being challenged and persuaded.

I remember being in awe of his assiduous approach to the preparatory work for Mafikeng. Over the course of 1996 and 1997, I had watched Mbeki become more hands-on and pragmatic than other comrade in the NEC and tripartite alliance leadership. But I had also watched him rise as a thorough and ruminative African intellectual, leading the ANC into a brand-new era of governing the country. Sitting at the ANC headquarters, I felt at home not just in the party but, for the first time, in an emerging democracy under Mbeki's astute stewardship.

With this bitterly divisive battle raging at Mafikeng, the drafting team straddled the chasm between liberation movement and government as a significant bridge between the past and a future that Mbeki and those around him were beginning to articulate.

IT WAS IN THIS heady atmosphere that I set to work with other technocrats and intellectuals made up of a formidable mix of stalwarts and younger members. Joel Netshitenzhe, David Makhura, Febe Potgieter, Naph Manana, Kenneth Creamer, Michael Sachs, Steyn Speed and others reflected a diligent approach to our work as scribes and interlocutors in various party commissions at Mafikeng. Under the astute leadership of Jeff Radebe, the team had developed a camaraderie, taking pride in the historic role we were playing in the flurry of policy activity that marked this stage of the transition. We worked long hours in the build-up to Mafikeng when, many will recall, Cyril Ramaphosa moved out of the ANC secretariat and active politics and into business, and Mbeki became the uncontested candidate to succeed Mandela as president of the Republic in 1999.

Though not a policy-making committee, we were to play an important role in substantively rearticulating the language and tenor of a liberation organisation that still talked of the National Democratic Revolution, on one hand, but was a governing party operating with a different set of rules, on the other. That wasn't an easy task. I was all too aware that liberation movements are driven by grand visions, and the ANC was no exception. But the leap from liberation to government meant a scaling back of radical ideals. Thus, I shared the conviction of Mbeki that the RDP had to be downscaled, with its champions at Mafikeng claiming not grand victories but small advances. In this environment it was little wonder that contending ideologies and interests between factions in the ANC-led alliance, principally the Cosatu–SACP bloc and Mbeki, came to mark the battle at Mafikeng.

It was a seminal moment, for it would shape the anatomy of post-apartheid politics for the next three decades, and the drafting team was deeply involved. Perhaps it was a measure of our role as scribes and interlocutors in commissions during a time of profound policy shifts that we were, unofficially, straddling prickly egos and hard lines. In retrospect, I do not doubt my intuition then that beneath the ideological battle, our role was to take some of the emotions out of the equation in the drafting process and present something more palatable to market forces, to the international community and to the expectant citizens of South Africa.

Mafikeng ended with Mbeki securely in the driving seat of the party and government. In public, there was consensus on GEAR as the strategic growth and development path for the country; but I think the moment the alliance partners walked out of Mafikeng, the consensus was broken. It would turn out to be the beginning of a faction fight, far more audacious than I could have imagined at first, by Mbeki's detractors to take over the country.

LOOKING BACK, WE may have been technocrats, but it would be an oversimplification to suggest that we were above the battle of ideas. We watched and debated, through the 1990s, as the battle brought a string of new headlines and charges by the ANC's labour allies against the neoliberal framework in which GEAR was located. Mbeki would often become furious at the growing discord and throw himself into blistering broadsides against Cosatu and the SACP. And who could blame him? The Mafikeng conference had, after all, reached a consensus, and now the partners were at each other's throats. He knew all too well that winning a debate on the conference floor was one thing, but the historical streams of support through which ANC membership coursed and crossed over into membership of Cosatu and the SACP made it difficult, if not impossible, at that early stage of the transition, to jettison the left.

A sort of turning point was reached at the end of Mandela's presidency in 1998 when Mbeki, exasperated by growing discord in the tripartite alliance, told the SACP at its conference at Crown Mines that year that if it wanted to pursue its socialist ambitions it was free to pursue the socialist revolution on its own. Mbeki's irritation with the SACP was apparent from author Malcolm Ray's observation at the conference of "no less than nine pejoratives, in quick succession, in Mbeki's lashing of the SACP".[21] "He was visibly agitated," Ray said to me, "and in no uncertain terms told the party leadership and delegates, in the presence of international guests from Cuba, that if it did not want to leave the tripartite alliance it would have to fall in line with GEAR as the official policy of the ANC and government."

Mbeki's public rebuke of the SACP brought an intensity to his anti-SACP crusade that would reach a final, climatic confrontation between the ANC's labour allies, mobilised around the personality of Jacob Zuma, on one side, and Mbeki's ANC, on the other, at the Polokwane conference in 2007. As the focus of public attention turned to the standoff between Mbeki and Zuma, of real concern to us in the drafting team was the economic agenda. A few of us in the team felt betrayed and excluded because, until that moment, there had been a consistent and sensible economic policy that, despite falling short of meeting growth and employment targets, had been able to extinguish the country's debt and replenish our foreign currency reserves to a respectable level, which was about $40 billion plus and growing at the time of Mbeki's departure from government.

As part of the drafting team, I responded to the crusading spirit at Polokwane with the same visceral antipathy to what seemed to be a double-edged message of economic radicalisation and anti-Mbeki-ism. I had grown up in ANC reading groups during my youth, where the teachings of Marx, Engels and Lenin were a staple diet of radical literature under conditions of apartheid oppression and illegality. But Marxism was never an ideology I embraced. At Polokwane I was deeply troubled by the push by the Zuma-led Cosatu–SACP–ANC Youth League axis for radical policy shifts that became a mobilising platform for Mbeki's removal from the West Wing and for Zuma's Radical Economic Transformation (RET) juggernaut.

In fact, the tumultuous build-up to Polokwane was such a clean sweep that there was very little time to debate policy. Once I read the policy recommendations by Cosatu and the SACP in the drafting team, I realised that this was a political game-changer. But I didn't realise quite how it would change the country, not because of the left-wing rhetoric about economic policy but because of the insatiable ambition of the Zuma faction.

THE START OF THE conference had all the hallmarks of a coup. I remember, clearly, the stifling atmosphere in the plenary hall. I was on the conference floor when the chairperson of the ANC, Patrick Lekota, who was widely perceived to be in the Mbeki camp, tried to address delegates. There was hissing from the back of the hall by a delegate dressed in Zulu regalia carrying a shield and spear and performing a Zulu dance. Others wore T-shirts with Zuma's face on the front. At the back of the t-shirts were the words "100 percent Zulu". My comrade and friend Wally Serote recalled to me the day he and a friend arrived at the conference venue when he observed a vendor outside wearing this T-shirt and he inquired where he had obtained it. To which Wally said the boy responded, "From some of the comrades inside, sir." This, says Wally, was already a very worrying phenomenon to him because as far as he was concerned, this ANC of ours had not promoted or advocated tribalism of any sort over its century-long history.

As a drafting team we experienced first-hand the complete withdrawal from policy and debate. As the days progressed, I recall the tangled mess of the commissions we were tasked with facilitating. We pretended we could still form commissions, but there was no interest from the branch and provincial delegates. I recall at one commission where I was a scribe eight NEC delegates being present without a single branch or provincial delegate. I was asked to go out and get people to come in. When I invited two young men to join the commission, they dangled a bottle of alcohol they were drinking. When I stressed the importance of the commission, they shifted their tone, laughing and declaring their support for Zuma. "We are here to vote for Zuma," they retorted. "Policy conference [six months earlier] took care of policy discussions," they insisted. The alliance assembled around Zuma at Polokwane had come to the conference with one goal: they had decided that it was time for Mbeki to go. That was all there was to it. No discussions were needed.

Equally bizarre was the significant presence of business and business lobbyists. That was the start of money playing a role in influencing voting, I think.

But through the turmoil of the five days and the decade that followed the consolidation of the RET faction around Zuma's state capture agenda, one thing that held things together was the drafting team. We were united behind the historical vision of the ANC and tried, in very difficult circumstances, to deal with the closing down of space in an attempt to keep a semblance of policy sanity amid the reckless radicalism of Zuma's ANC. We were convinced that it was necessary to keep a check on the form and tenor of policy resolutions so that we did not scare off investors. At Polokwane, that was no mean feat. It fell on us to make sense of policy conference decisions taken six months earlier by refining them into coherent and sensible resolutions. It was our attempt to save the conference from complete disaster. It was a job that summoned all our skill in repairing broken policies so as to give them a modicum of respectability at Polokwane.

The truth is that the format of the conference, arranged by an external service provider, was designed to control the policy narrative. Either they did not understand the culture of the ANC or their design of the conference hall, like an executive boardroom with 4,000 microphones at every delegate seat instead of a roving mike, was intended to allow Zuma backers free rein to disrupt the proceedings. The minute I saw this I knew it was going to be monumental disaster. And as things turned out, the chair had no control over inputs or noisy disruptions from the floor. By the end of the plenary, Lekota had all but given up.

To his credit, it was ANC secretary general Kgalema Motlanthe, widely seen as a rational interlocutor, who tried to bring order to the chaos. When things went pear-shaped, it was Motlanthe who appealed for calm. My strong bond with him as a comrade and mentor began when I became an employee at the ANC headquarters around the time of his election as secretary general at Mafikeng. Because he served two terms as SG, he was elected at Polokwane as deputy president. Technically, he was my boss at Luthuli House until I left in 2000. Through the chaos of Polokwane, I had been consulting with Motlanthe about policy issues we had to deal with in the drafting team. He knew my political views and trusted me. In the end, however, the gap between a party in government and the sudden resurgence of a radical liberation movement struggle ethos was a bridge too far for the drafting team.

It was hard to see through the fog of state capture then, but what would become clearer over the years is that talk of "radical economic transformation", which would include calls after the 2012 conference at Mangaung for nationalising the Reserve Bank and land expropriation without compensation, was only really a pretext for the brazen populism of a faction quietly working as an oligarchy in the Union Buildings after

Mbeki's removal. In reality, talk of radicalism was only really a pretext for what would become state capture.

It was a bruising time that inflamed tempers in the ANC, where the Mbeki name had become synonymous with neoliberalism and centralised power. It was a time when a shadowy world emerged of shifting alliances and misinformation peddlers – no doubt instigated by the Zuma faction – plotting labyrinthine conspiracies, and talk of splits and breakaway parties was reaching fever pitch. I did not support splits in the party.

When, in the wake of Polokwane, Lekota eventually formed the Congress of the People (COPE) in response to Mbeki's removal, I did not support the move. As far as I was concerned, this was a speedbump along a long journey. As with Zuma's ascendancy, I felt that COPE was a petulant but nonetheless minor deflection from the ANC's vision and historical mission to fight for social justice and eliminate the vast inequalities created by apartheid and, ultimately, build a common patriotism.

I had by that time left for England to pursue my doctoral studies. The appearance of the ANC's dissolution under Zuma's leadership was difficult to stomach, but distance brings a sense of proportion, and I remained true to the ANC, partly because I understood that the ANC, like all living political organisations, can adjust to large moments that throughout its history have triggered divergent tendencies in its ranks.

From my perch in Cambridge, I was able to see more clearly that the Polokwane moment was no different from the 1940s when a radical faction led by the ANC Youth League attempted to gain ascendancy in the party, or from the late 1950s when a group of African nationalists challenged the party's dominance by whites in the Communist Party and eventually broke away to form the Pan Africanist Congress (PAC), led by Robert Sobukwe. Through all this, however, the ANC always held a moderate social democratic position. It had survived, and grown. There was nothing to suggest to me that the Zuma-led coup at Polokwane was any different.

UPON MY RETURN TO South Africa, preparations for the 2010 Soccer World Cup were in full swing, along with corruption around World

Cup tenders. The Zuma administration was also in full swing. After a two-year interlude in Cape Town, I moved back to Johannesburg where I began reconnecting with comrades in the party just as we were preparing for the 2012 national centenary conference at Mangaung, where the ANC had been launched in 1912.

With Mbeki and his allies exiled from the party, I had by this time thrown my support behind the party's deputy president Kgalema Motlanthe against Zuma. I met with him on several occasions to try to convince him to stand for party president, but Motlanthe, ever the diplomat, would not express himself openly. He told me on more than one occasion that he did not want to promote factionalism in the party. "The only way to break factionalism", he once told me, "was not to be part of one." I replied with a question: "If factionalism was the problem, then why was he not standing up to Zuma?" He understood my argument and began to see the importance of people outside the ANC knowing that there were alternative choices to Zuma. "It's important to say there are capable leaders in the ANC that can take over," he said. It was a clinching argument. Against his instincts to stay out of the faction fight, he decided to stand.

In the months leading to Mangaung, I threw my energy into mobilising support for Motlanthe. My first tangible act was my own party branch in the Johannesburg suburb of Craighall. Even though I was secretary of the Yeoville branch in the 1990s, I had not been in a leadership position until 2012, when I became an ANC branch executive member again. I wanted to be a voting delegate in 2012. That's how strongly I felt about defeating Zuma and his ilk.

By this time there was a discernible current of nationalism coursing through the RET as a modus operandi. The big man politics of the Premier League, with Ace Magashule at its helm, began to emerge as a mobilising tool in some of the provinces. They had by this time become the final arbiters of government tenders in the provinces. A loose coalition thus emerged around this time, with Zuma its centre of gravity.

In this poisonous milieu, we did not stand a chance. Not only was the control of tenders a way in which to dispense patronage, but the Premier League manipulated numbers to ensure delegates at

Mangaung would vote for Zuma. It was a time of despondency when our comrades began to think that we had lost the ANC to mafia tendencies in leadership at all levels of the party and government. I remember an anecdote in Mpumalanga about conference organisers buying KFC chicken for delegates as a way of buying Zuma votes. It was patronage politics at its most base level.

It was the first time, since Polokwane, that lawfare emerged as a disruptive mechanism. When Songezo Mjongile from the Western Cape stood up to urge delegates from the Free State, who were embroiled in court cases and interdicts over corruption, to leave the hall so that other delegates could discuss their electoral status without intimidation, Zuma backers shot the proposal down. That opened a flank for a rowdy discussion that reached a climax a full three hours later. It was resolved that the Free State delegation would remain in the hall. The fact that they stayed was the first indication that Zuma's camp had the numbers. From there, the rest of the conference was a downhill slide for the Motlanthe camp.

By the end of the discussion on credentials it was clear to me that we would not be able to claw our way out of the chaos. Not only did the Zuma camp have the numbers, but there was something alien to the ANC that emerged. An even stronger streak of ethno-nationalism than at Polokwane began to surface around Zuma. I was familiar with traditional ANC songs, and when I asked some comrades why I had not heard the songs being sung by delegates before, they said it was because they were traditional Inkatha Freedom Party (IFP) songs that had been slightly tweaked to align with the ANC. They were being sung by IFP members who flocked to Zuma's ANC after his victory at Polokwane. When Zuma delivered his presidential address, he opened with a church hymn rather than a traditional ANC song. This, too, was something new.

Meanwhile, the RET faction was cementing its policy agenda.

IF POLOKWANE WAS a mishmash of neoliberal and left-wing policies, Mangaung was a 180 degree turn to nationalisation as the policy premise of the RET. One by one, delegates in commissions argued for the nationalisation of the Reserve Bank and the expropriation of land without compensation. It was a very difficult time for the drafting team, who were now being asked to break with traditional policy.

Within the team, there was a great deal of debate over the policy shift, led by Tito Mboweni, Joel Netshitenzhe and Kenneth Creamer. We spent hours grappling with the implications of RET policies in an attempt to make sense of the proposal to nationalise the Reserve Bank and of the rejection by RET delegates of the market-led "willing buyer, willing seller" principle behind the county's land redistribution policy. There were debates about the constitutionality of both policy positions, which, we recall, became a chestnut in parliament after Mangaung. When leading members of the team tried to explain to the conference that the proposals would not pass the constitutionality test, the RET camp would not listen. They wanted us to make the proposals sensible and palatable enough for people outside conference to stomach. It was our job as a team, not to make policy but to refine it, and we obliged.

Once he had sailed through the first five years of his presidency without major glitches, Zuma's second term would mark yet another tipping point. Having won at Mangaung and pushed through RET policy positions, the Zuma administration became more emboldened, with talk of a "second transition" towards radical socio-economic transformation. The ANC's contestation of the 2014 general election may have carried the whiff of an ostensibly radical agenda, but it was in truth an attempt to rally popular support behind state capture in all but name.

And so, the period between 2012 and 2017, when the ANC held its 54th national conference at Nasrec, was nothing short of disastrous. Corruption under the now infamous Gupta oligarchy became more blatant and systemic. By 2016, I had pinned my hopes on Ramaphosa's candidacy at Nasrec. It was around this time that I decided that one of the ways I wanted to make a contribution to his campaign was by writing columns ahead of the conference. For the first time, I began openly criticising the ANC leadership.

There were those in the party who felt that I was washing the party's dirty linen in public, but there was an even larger group of comrades who appreciated what I was doing because they did not have the nerve to openly ask prickly questions. They would, instead, privately WhatsApp me with congratulatory comments. There were, on the other hand, very senior comrades who thought otherwise. Deputy secretary general Jessie Duarte would sometimes write privately to me accusing me of falsehoods. It was a sacred covenant among Zuma's cronies to dismiss as lies anything that publicly impugned them.

But pesky responses did not bother me. The majority of comrades in the party and government were reading my columns, and I was satisfied that negative reactions seemed to accumulate in inverse proportion to the praise I got. On the whole, they appreciated that I was speaking truth to power. I'd often run into them at social gatherings. Most would commend me. Some issued stern warnings, sometimes laced with threats to kill me. I was, after all, threatening not only Zuma, but their own lifelines to his patronage. I was advocating a return to the ANC we had lost in 2007, when Mbeki was ousted. And now I was pushing Ramaphosa's candidacy, a billionaire, to be sure, who could not be lured by corruption. I was also ranging my guns against Ace Magashule, by openly calling for a clampdown on the Premier League.

Whether my columns helped the outcome of the 2017 conference is hard to tell. But whatever the impact of our propaganda campaign, what matters, I think, is that by the time we went to Nasrec Zuma was embattled, embroiled in loud calls to impeach him over his abuse of taxpayers' money to upgrade his Nkandla private homestead. The RET faction, while not defeated, was in tired retreat. Its resource smash and grab was coming to an end.

The RET's defeat by a narrow margin at Nasrec and Zuma's resignation as president of the Republic in February 2018 seemed to presage the final extinction of the RET. It was a short walk to the 55th conference at Nasrec in 2022.

Or so I thought ...

Two
A perfect storm

Sometime in February 2017 I got a call from a comrade I had come to know during my involvement in the student movement. On the phone was Steyn Speed, who had gone on to become Cyril Ramaphosa's presidential speechwriter. It was a time when the ravages of state capture were in plain view. For close to a decade, Jacob Zuma had hollowed out the state, treating state-owned enterprises like his private ATM machine. So pervasive was the parade of looting that ordinary citizens and investors were left feeling helpless and hopeless.

Through the years of Zuma's presidency, and later during Ramaphosa's election campaign for the presidency of the ANC at Nasrec in December 2017, journalists became beacons of hope for society. I mention this because they were not only civil society's last line of defence against corruption and a collapsing state, but also influential spokespersons for society's aspirations. If media is a theatre of an important part of normal political life, journalists brought daring and gusto to the country's politics. It is not an overstatement to say that people looked to the media as the most reliable interpreters of their hopes. In contrast to the grey, tractable pro-Zuma Independent Newspapers media group, a handful of feisty online publications like *GroundUp* and, most notably, the *Daily Maverick* sprang up over the years.

Inspired by the hope Ramaphosa had developed as a central theme in his State of the Nation speech in 2019, I began writing a regular column for the *Daily Maverick* in which I openly countered his detractors in the ideological war to define Ramaphosa's ANC. Over time my columns would earn me the appellation in the ANC and media of an "intellectual provocateur". Publicly, it was overblown and a little embarrassing; privately and in comradely circles, I was quite proud of it. What was needed, I felt, was a critical voice in the public domain, but one which displayed a sensitive grasp of the ANC's history, its founding mission and moral supremacy, and an awareness of the complex challenges confronting Ramaphosa's presidency.

Naturally, given their enthusiastic promotion of Ramaphosa's candidacy, the articles caught the eye of Steyn Speed. He wanted to meet me for a drink and chat about my columns. Speed was a seasoned political operator and moderate reformer who shared my enthusiasm for Ramaphosa's measured temperament and embrace of a market-driven reconstruction of the economy. The stakes in early 2018 were enormous and real. Ramaphosa may have just succeeded in banishing Zuma from power and edging out his RET acolytes at the 2017 ANC conference, but the chaotic surge of events during Zuma's nine-year reign had left the country and market deeply unsettled and unsure whether the ANC was fit to govern.

Perception, it is said, is nine-tenths of reality and the ANC had become synonymous with an entire economic system which, until that point, was rigged to reward the bad and punish the good. The only winners were corrupt officials in Zuma's ANC and government.

WHEN, IN FEBRUARY 2017, I eventually met Speed a few weeks after the opening of parliament, there was a sense of unreality in the air. It was at once unimaginable and brimming with expectations that, finally, an economy felled by Zuma could be rebuilt.

I had got to know Speed as an activist, and over the years he and I had shared some profound assumptions about the economy, the state and the ANC. The mood during our conversation was exhilarating but tempered by the prevailing reality: the factional war in the ANC and government had forced us to play hardball; it crushed those who did not conform to the rules of the game. This would become the standard version of a propaganda war. For all the revelry in the heady onrush of the country's post-Zuma statehood, the country was an uncontrolled jungle of Zuma acolytes who, still bitter from their patron's defeat, were angling to make a comeback at the ANC's 2017 conference. They were thinking about destroying Ramaphosa in order to recapture the state, not rebuild it.

The threat was real, and Speed needed a trusted ally who would counter attempts by the RET to spread mischief and discredit Ramaphosa ahead of the ANC national conference in December 2017, and advance his reconstruction agenda on the campaign trail.

It is not unreasonable to assume that Ramaphosa, a realist, must have been under no illusions that the journey from economic and moral ruin would have to stretch a thousand yards through treacherous minefields. The heart of the challenge was economic, but its blood and muscle were an intellectual and moral battle to win hearts and minds. It was in that space that Speed, as Ramaphosa's speechwriter, had developed a powerful niche within the presidency. Speaking bluntly, he told me that a bold battle of ideas in the public domain was needed to avoid the quagmire of politics that led to Mbeki's ousting in 2007. It was strategically important to shine a spotlight on Ramaphosa's vision for the country in the build-up to Nasrec.

I did not need convincing. I knew that, with the ANC's image severely tarnished and just about every media organisation opposed to it, the window for a progressive counter-narrative in the public sphere was closing. More balanced media platforms like the *Daily Maverick* had understandably taken a very dim view of corruption under Zuma's ANC, while *Maverick*'s rival, Independent Newspapers, owned by Iqbal Survé, had very publicly opposed Ramaphosa and, in 2017, openly came out in support of Zuma's presidential candidate, Nkosazana Dlamini-Zuma.

Always a fountain of ideas, Speed had given me a task that re-animated me; there was now more focused attention on a campaign to advance Cyril Ramaphosa's presidential ambitions. I gladly accepted the role. And so, on that February evening over drinks, I entered

President Cyril Ramaphosa's battle of ideas as one of his unofficial spin doctors. My first real test was to counter attempts by the RET in the party to spread misinformation and propaganda to weaken Ramaphosa's credibility and authority. We wasted no time discussing my next column, which appeared in the *Daily Maverick* under the headline "South Africa: Cyril, Gordhan et al, and the Gordian knot".[22]

THROUGHOUT 2022, MY weekly columns had grown more blusterous. Sometimes I advanced Ramaphosa's policies, sometimes I vigorously lashed out at RET propaganda and dirty tricks on the campaign trail. These were strange days marked by perilous economic conditions and menacing smear campaigns. When it came to the ANC's reputation, I did not deign to airbrush the primal wound that had developed since Zuma took the reins. I saw my writing as nothing less than an attempt to redeem the party by promoting a sort of revivalist orientation towards the ANC's vision and mission that Ramaphosa had begun to articulate in his policies and public utterances.

A central theme in my arguments was that while Zuma and his cohorts in the RET were tainted, this did not mean that the ANC was, by implication, painted with the same brush. My job was to shine a torch through the fog of despair in the battle between rival factions and, ultimately, swing public sentiment towards Ramaphosa as the best hope for the party and country. My columns were criticised by many readers but were generally well received. The thought in my mind around this time was that criticism was better than no response. What mattered was that I was being read. There may have been some intellectual jousting, but more important was for readers to see Ramaphosa as an agent of change and a wide broom to sweep out the muck of the Zuma era.

Months later, in mid-December 2017, our campaign finally came together at the Nasrec Expo Centre, where Ramaphosa came face to face with RET candidate Nkosazana Dlamini-Zuma at the party's 54th national conference. Having won the battle for the ANC by a whisker of a margin, Ramaphosa emerged from that conference with a mandate to shift policy from the bizarre, self-destructive RET agenda back to the centre where it belonged. I was delighted and felt that our campaign was moving smoothly. Here, finally, was our comeuppance after the Polokwane coup. We had succeeded in pushing a moderate agenda to centre stage and kicking out the reckless delusions of the RET to nationalise strategic centres of economic power like the Reserve Bank. There was also a new energy in the drafting team. We agreed among ourselves on certain unwritten rules: no racist talk of attacking white monopoly capital. Instead, we sought to discuss and debate the challenge of a "skewed economy".

Behind the scenes, however, the Zuma faction was not interested in being sore losers. As 2018 dawned, the ensuing political melee quickly demonstrated that the RET's extremist agitations had an alarmingly wide measure of support. No sooner had the ANC conference ended than there was resistance to parliamentary pressure to impeach Zuma. Barely a week after the ANC conference in December, the Constitutional Court dropped a bombshell in a ruling that parliament had failed in its duty to hold Zuma to account for state-funded upgrades to his Nkandla estate.[23] In the same ruling the court ordered the National Assembly to urgently make rules that allowed Zuma to be impeached for violating the Constitution by refusing to pay back public money.[24]

I will always vividly remember that celebratory moment when I got the news. I was waiting anxiously for the outcome of a scheduled parliamentary no-confidence vote on 15 February, which, we recall, had been a ritual affair in opposition party attempts to impeach Zuma. In a broadcast to the nation on the evening of 14 February, Zuma resigned from the presidency before the end of his second term. By a majority vote, parliament moved swiftly to elect Ramaphosa to the presidency. It felt as if I had emerged from a decade of darkness into the golden sunlight of a new dawn. I was ecstatic, as were my comrades in the Ramaphosa camp. I have no doubt that, in a small way, our propaganda campaign to rescue the ANC and advance Cyril Ramaphosa's presidential ambitions had contributed to that moment.

AT JUST THAT MOMENT, in the midst of a seismic shift in the balance of power, I got a call from Marion Sparg, who was Ramaphosa's communications guru. Sparg was a pragmatic, smart comrade with a long activist history who felt that my columns had consistently kept the candle burning. She needed someone who would help write Ramaphosa's speeches in order to bolster the party's campaign for the 2019 elections. I was honoured and, without batting an eyelid, accepted. By this time there were two defining strands to my columns. The first was directed at the president; the second appealed to an exasperated white electorate who had been alienated by Zuma's talk of white monopoly capital and radical economic transformation. My aim was to win them over to Ramaphosa's cause. I wanted to demonstrate, in words, that Ramaphosa was, in deeds, committed to rebuilding the economic and social fabric of a nation torn apart by Zuma. It was to be a call for unity in a collaborative endeavour to rebuild South Africa.

The political melee in the months leading to the 2019 elections was fuelled, simultaneously, by the anger of the RET faction and the desire of Ramaphosa's ANC for a new era. But for the latter to succeed, those involved in the looting frenzy of the Zuma era had to be investigated and brought to book. The issue was in fact much more profound: South Africa had become a state without functioning institutions and functioning rules of the game. Its previous rulers were indifferent to, and complicit in, the chaos.

Worried about the disorder, Ramaphosa knew that rebuilding state institutions was not going to be possible without first dealing with those implicated in corruption within the very same state institutions which he needed to pioneer his vision. His first act, therefore, was to move swiftly in giving effect to the Zondo Commission of Enquiry into State Capture, headed by Judge Raymond Zondo, in late 2018, much to the elation of the majority of South Africans. Here, for the first time, was evidence of tangible moves to deal with corruption in the state. Ramaphosa's government declared that the calamity that had befallen the nation was not the work of one misfit or family, but a network of individuals in the state and private sector. The Zondo Commission was thus given a wide remit to conduct its inquiry, without fear or favour.

But as the curtain fell on 2018, Ramaphosa's reform agenda was still a matter of great uncertainty for citizens and investors alike. He might have defeated Zuma and the RET at Nasrec, but only by a slender margin. As far as business was concerned, Ramaphosa was tainted by association with a corrupt party leadership.

THE YEAR 2019 BEGAN at the most volatile point along the inexorable curve of the post-apartheid transition. There was a pungent air of ferment across the country when, in February, Ramaphosa stood before a broken nation and delivered a State of the Nation speech that would turn out to be his best performance yet. He surely knew that it was his first and last chance to instil hope in a country reeling from years of state madness and corruption. He had just faced the most cunning and dirty politician in high office since 1994, and won. The economic and political devastation of the "Zupta" oligarchy produced a new vision of the government's role under Ramaphosa, one that seemed to circle back to the moral symbolism of the Mandela years and the economic rationality of Thabo Mbeki's government. I remember the sense of pride I felt when I watched the president implore all South Africans to rally around a "new dawn"; to tell oneself, "Tuma Mina": I want to be there to do my part for my country. The legendary song by Bra Hugh Masekela reverberated throughout the country. There was hope again.

The speech was not anything like the reckless banter of radical economic transformation that made citizens and investors jittery. And in contrast to his predecessor, his speech instantly marked Ramaphosa out as a man with a patriotic and proprietary sense of South Africa. It was a ringing address designed to purge the ANC's public image of state capture. Embroidered with unity and hope as central themes, it sought to tap a latent vein of hope in the ANC and country against a backdrop of deep divisions in society.

"This is the year in which we will turn the tide of corruption in our public institutions. We are determined to build a society defined by decency and integrity, that does not tolerate the plunder of public resources, nor the theft by corporate criminals of the hard-earned savings of ordinary people,"[25] he told his listening audience, to wide applause.

When he concluded the speech, there was a sense across a broad political spectrum of a man with large ambitions: Ramaphosa's most important message was his determination to break the stranglehold of Zuma's backers on the state, deploying his energy to a campaign crafted around putting the enormous resources of the country back into public hands.

Behind the crafting of the speech was the hand of Steyn Speed, who was clearly more than Ramaphosa's speechwriter. He skilfully and dutifully grounded Ramaphosa's social democratic conscience in the ANC's goals. And he knew exactly how to give Ramaphosa's vision wings. When the pomp and ceremony were over, the message of a "new dawn" had the intended effect: Ramaphosa's call for collective action to rebuild the country did, in fact, tap a vein of hope.

With such an undertaking, however, Ramaphosa faced a recurring problem: the devastation of the Covid-19 pandemic and the search by residual Zuma loyalists in the RET faction of the party for vulnerabilities in his administration. In the midst of an unnerving pandemic, for a perfect storm threatened the Ramaphosa administration when his opponents, either by design or coincidence, staged their biggest fightback since their defeat in December 2017.

In July 2021, a catastrophic wave of riots sent shock waves through the country and foreign investment community, whom Ramaphosa had just made a point of wooing to his foreign investment cause. In the months after his election, he wasted no time assembling a team of emissaries, including former finance minister Trevor Manuel, to crisscross the world with a single mission: to mobilise capital markets and promote South Africa as a foreign direct investment destination. Now, the forces of good and evil seemed to be arrayed against one another, in a battle that came close to an earth-shattering climax. Many in the country, outraged and petrified at the same time, muttered darkly that the riots were an attempted insurrection instigated by the RET, many of whom were heavily implicated in state capture. All the while, attacks on Ramaphosa's credibility grew, though they were contained within acceptable limits. There was always tantalising poisonous gossip.

The riots were eventually quelled, but the months that followed brought more decline as the country careered towards bureaucratic incompetence and corruption in the public sector. No longer suspended in a succession of lockdowns that had universalised the global economic carnage, the ANC and government under Ramaphosa confronted their first true test. While Ramaphosa's Economic Reconstruction and Recovery Plan did not include a complete overhaul of the economic policy framework that had been adopted in 2010 by the Zuma administration, what set his leadership apart from the previous administration was a plan that sought to align the country's post-Covid recovery with a just energy transition to a new green economy.

But it was not until a year later that Ramaphosa faced his second real test: rolling blackouts began devastating the economy, reaching their highest point since 2008 in mid-2022, when households and businesses experienced more than ten hours of load-shedding every day. The country was seething with discontent, but the deepest source of discontent was rotten leadership.

IN REACTION TO THE crisis, Ramaphosa ramped up his just energy transition plan and by mid-2022 introduced the national Energy Action Plan, promising far-reaching changes to energy production. But the problem lay partly in looting and partly in gross incompetence at Eskom, which had run the power utility aground. All the while, Ramaphosa's reforms, which were long-term, sustainable solutions, were understandably a matter of great uncertainty. Fast-paced crises and mounting public pressure to end load-shedding now left Ramaphosa and his government reeling.

In this atmosphere, the media became a barometer of growing frustration and anger among small businesses and households baying for blood. To the media, all the talk of an economic recovery and energy transition without immediate practical interventions was deeply unsettling. They blamed the ANC. They blamed the government. And who could disagree with them? With rolling blackouts battering the economy and no tangible short-term interventions to resolve the problem, the country once again seemed adrift.

By the time the blackouts had reached a peak, in mid-2022, of ten hours of load-shedding a day, a number of media commentators and journalists began to doubt the president's political will to solve the problem. Embattled by the impact of blackouts on households and businesses, people were furious. The real story is that Ramaphosa's solution just wouldn't do it. They were not buying Ramaphosa's long-term plan and scathingly attacked the ANC and government for ignoring the crisis. They wanted answers and solutions and went so far as to argue that South Africa needed a strong political leader to deal with the crisis at Eskom. Ramaphosa, they felt, was incapable of rising to the challenge. Of course, this was patently untrue.

Around mid-January 2023, just as Ramaphosa was preparing to depart for the World Economic Forum (WEF) in Davos, Switzerland, the *Sowetan* newspaper ran a hard-hitting front-page article on the crippling impact of load-shedding on small businesses.[26] Ramaphosa immediately cancelled his Davos trip to deal with the energy bottleneck at the heart of the economic crisis. Writing in his weekly address to the nation, *From the desk of the President*, he acknowledged the *Sowetan*'s article, which had gone so far as to list the small businesses that had gone under:

> As loadshedding continues to wreak havoc on businesses, households and communities, the last thing South Africans want to hear are excuses or unrealistic promises. The demands for an immediate end to power cuts are wholly understandable. Everyone is fed up ... Though it may be easy to blame our present woes on dysfunctionality at Eskom, a combination of factors have contributed to the crisis. It is important to recall the reasons for the current situation so that our response tackles the causes of our crisis, not just the symptoms. Lack of investment in new generating capacity, poor power plant maintenance, corruption and criminality, sabotage of infrastructure, rising municipal debt and a lack of suitable skills at Eskom have all created a perfect storm. We should not make the mistakes of the past. For many years, critical maintenance was deferred, and our power stations were run too hard in order to keep the lights on. As a country, we are now paying the price for these miscalculations. We must be realistic about our challenges and about what it is going to take to fix them. While we all desperately want to, we cannot end load-shedding overnight.[27]

During subsequent meetings with representatives of labour and business, traditional leaders, religious leaders, premiers, metro mayors and leaders of political parties, Ramaphosa stressed the importance of "staying the course" instead of coming up with unsustainable short-term solutions. He said the national Energy Action Plan, which aimed to improve the performance of Eskom's power stations, remained the most realistic path towards ending load-shedding. "As we know only too well from the experience of the last few weeks, many of the measures in the plan will not be felt in the immediate term," he said. "That is why we are using every means at our disposal, calling on every resource we have, to get power onto the grid as a matter of extreme urgency."

The message: there were no quick fixes. South Africans had to buckle up and ride out the load-shedding storm. It was not what the leaders he spoke to and ordinary South Africans wanted to hear, but it is what they got. It was a message that was hard to swallow.

MUCH HAS BEEN WRITTEN about Ramaphosa's aloofness since his 2022 State of the Nation (Sona) address. Widely perceived as a far cry from the energy and passion of his first Sona speech in 2019, many media commentators have given their critical assessments of his performance, accusing him of not living up to his promises. Even former president Thabo Mbeki joined the chorus, openly criticising Ramaphosa for not having a plan to respond to South Africa's economic challenges.[28]

But what Ramaphosa surely knew from his own hard-won experience in the trenches of politics and business was that the answers to South Africa's problems were not going to come out of textbooks. His 2022 Sona speech may have lacked the lyricism and popular allure of his "new dawn" address in 2019, but he gave details of the challenges faced by his government, new and old.

Among the new was the challenge of economic recovery from the Covid-19 pandemic and, of course, the economic impact of load-shedding. He heaped praises on the Solidarity Fund set up to cope with the pandemic, including contributions by about 300,000 individuals and 300 companies. "This, perhaps, gives a proper background to the kind of response the government can marshal against the problems of the country," he said.[29] Then he went on to list old challenges that faced the country:

> The key task of government is to create the conditions that will enable the private sector – both big and small – to emerge, to grow, to access new markets, to create new products, and to hire more employees. The problems in the economy are deep and they are structural ... When electricity supply cannot be guaranteed, when railways and ports are inefficient, when innovation is held back by a scarcity of broadband spectrum, when water quality deteriorates, companies are reluctant to invest and the economy cannot function properly.[30]

The problems, in other words, were overwhelmingly structural. What he did not say, but no doubt knew, was that political power in South Africa was often brokered, votes were bought or stolen, and, in 2022, the outcome of the party leadership race would depend on corrupt practices. Eskom had become a feeding trough. But there was a new variable that had emerged in media reportage: corruption at Eskom now had the acrid whiff of sabotage. Either by design or coincidence, I suspected that this was one way to hamstring Ramaphosa's government, discredit his leadership and steal votes at Nasrec.

The mere hint of sabotage was a turning point that brought not only corruption but the modus operandi of Ramaphosa's opponents into sharp focus. More than just for the money, they may well have been engaged in a campaign to weaken Ramaphosa's chances at the ANC's 2022 national conference. Of course, there was no way of telling for sure. Lumbering out of the fog of chaos, suspicions of sabotage were expressed in some media reportage, but its true nature was hard to discern amid official statements by government that incompetence and neglect were larger factors.

THEN, JUST MONTHS before the ANC's 55th elective conference in December, the Ramaphosa administration faced another blow that was its most serious yet. The president was drawn into a messy scandal involving millions of US dollars allegedly stolen from his Phala Phala farmhouse in the Waterberg, Limpopo, by criminals. The markets immediately reacted to rumours that the scandal was large enough to force Ramaphosa's resignation. Markets don't like the unknown; with Ramaphosa gone, the unknown was the least of our worries. South Africa's history of corruption and gross political mismanagement is still fresh in investors' minds, as are the downgrades to subinvestment status as a result of the years of looting state coffers during Jacob Zuma's presidency.

It was such a bewildering moment that, even after a full-blown investigation into the currency fall, no one could identify a single compelling reason for why it happened. Historically, the currency had developed a habit, after long periods of stability, of heading into an outsized sell-off in reaction to adverse events. This meant that if the currency were to respond as sharply as it had in the past to a Ramaphosa resignation, the outcome could be an exchange rate of R20 to the dollar.[31]

For Ramaphosa to refute the allegations was, of course, like wrestling with monsters in a nightmare. The accusations became more and more unreal in their horror. They seemed premeditated, designed to thwart every rebuttal and, ultimately, derail his presidential campaign.

With a few months to go to the ANC's conference, it was tempting to believe media speculation that Phala Phala showed the hidden hand of the RET; that the scandal was a carefully orchestrated ploy to discredit the president or force his resignation. Indeed, Ramaphosa's spokesman told the media that the president was considering all options. Among these, no doubt, was his resignation.

The timing was impeccable. The facts of the story aside, I wondered who stood to gain from the exposé. For months afterwards, the president was the chief defendant *in absentia*, tried in the court of public opinion, which is just as his opponents must have intended. The RET now spoke of Ramaphosa's laundering of foreign currency and use of currency as a slush fund to buy votes ahead of the December conference. Zuma went so far as to allege that Ramaphosa had been a CIA agent working for the dismemberment of the party.[32]

As the days progressed and the media dug in, I set to work with other comrades in the Ramaphosa camp to defend our presidential candidate. It was a convulsive time. The market remained, stubbornly, a choppy sea of currency volatility and investor uncertainty. The whole atmosphere, I felt, called for sensitivity and courage. Once again, I saw my role as a spin doctor. And so I immediately set out to write a column in the president's defence. On 6 June, News24 ran an article by me under the headline "A case of wag the dog? Fraser will have to prove his claims".[33] In it I argued that the charges against the president, first revealed by the former spy chief Arthur Fraser, were an attempt to deflect attention from his successful campaign.

Of course, there was an avalanche of criticism in response to my column. The disorientation and panic among readers were distressing to see. It was easy, I surmised, to entertain the notion that money laundering accounted for the forex in Ramaphosa's Phala Phala home. My instinct, however, was to see the answers that the event had given us as far less clear-cut. I was trying to hold the line to manage the problem, and went on to argue, in response to criticism, that as far as the forex at Phala Phala was concerned, both the South African Revenue Service (SARS) and the Reserve Bank could, and should, be approached to resolve the matter if the concern was that the currency was undeclared. It was that simple. Again there was an outcry amid more vitriolic attacks against Ramaphosa, who was now accused of violating the Constitution.

At that time, I argued that not everyone could see through the fog, least of all opposition parties for whom Phala Phala signalled the end of Ramaphosa. Nowhere was media reportage, in the heat of a leadership contest, focused on Ramaphosa's achievements since Zuma's resignation. Far from the policy madness and unbridled looting of the Zuma era, Ramaphosa restored a semblance of policy coherence to the party. He took tangible steps to probe state capture. He kept the economy on a relatively even keel through some of the most historically difficult times for the country. He had allowed the Reserve Bank the freedom to raise interest rates, giving South Africa its best shot at quelling inflation. Under his leadership, public sector finances at last looked as if they were heading in the right direction, with the all-important primary budget surplus, when revenue exceeds non-interest spending, expected to be reached before schedule in 2023/4. He also made important headway in getting the infrastructure programme up and running – no mean feat in difficult economic conditions.

WHAT HAD GONE wrong? My conclusion was that the main preoccupation of the country with Phala Phala had done its worst: from the very moment the scandal broke, public attention was riveted by Ramaphosa's departure. It did not dawn on the media that there was no obvious successor who could put investors – and most South Africans – at ease about the future of the country. It was my attempt to draw attention to Ramaphosa's presidential claims.

But that was only partially true. The real story was that Ramaphosa's approach to the economic crisis backfired. By focusing on the unsustainability of quick fixes, he excluded large swathes of the population who perceived the absence of immediate interventions as the president's failure to act. Concerned about the damage to the economy and the direct impact on their lives, they now fell outside his sphere of influence. The Phala Phala scandal, combined with the surge in inflation which dug deep holes in the pockets of ordinary citizens, only served to heighten mistrust and uncertainty. The implications were huge. The cost of doing business was rising. Investment was grinding to a halt. Those who had the means were sending their money abroad, creating a river of "capital flight" out of South Africa.

By December 2022, Ramaphosa's resignation seemed almost inevitable. Then, after months of nerve-racking turmoil, he was persuaded by his backers in the NEC that he had the numbers to win the party presidency at Nasrec. As I watched Ramaphosa on the hustings during his campaign, I kept thinking that he was the right person for governing the country at the right time. It seemed to me that by the first week of December the worst was over. He now seemed ebullient about the conference and the party's prospects in the 2024 elections.

Just as hyperinflation began to roll through the economy, he started to think about the big picture. South Africa was a broken economy that needed to attract investment, build confidence in its currency and rebuild basic institutions of the state and the market. But first he had to get the ANC's own house in order; he had to renew the party. That was his message.

This yearning for hope was fertile ground for large ideas. The man to drive those ideas, I argued in my columns, was Ramaphosa. By the time of the December conference my candidate was in the driving seat. The RET, I surmised, must surely have felt a sense of impending doom. Their gambit to oust Ramaphosa had failed. The road to Nasrec was open.

Three

Helter-Skelter

It was a warm December afternoon, and I was having lunch at my home in Johannesburg. I was anxiously waiting to hear whether I would be a non-voting member of the drafting committee at the ANC's 55th conference in two days' time. The man with the key was the ANC's policy coordinator Spongy Moodley, but for months there was no word from him. Moodley, we recall, had appointed me to the resolutions and drafting committee in 1996 when I was a salaried employee at party headquarters. It was a role I had performed diligently and loyally at every ANC national elective conference since Mafikeng, and Nasrec was no different. Why, then, did I spend months waiting to be accredited?

On that December afternoon my suspicions turned to attempts by detractors of Cyril Ramaphosa to block my accreditation and attendance. I knew, in the build-up to the conference, that the accreditation process would become a key battleground for the RET faction in the contest for leadership positions.

It was a tense time, as patrons and power-brokers in the party knew quite well how to sway delegates. They could manipulate and circumvent the established rules of conference through behind-the-scenes deal-making with branch and provincial delegates and bribe their way to conference – and, eventually, power. It seemed like an all-or-nothing environment, with two opposing camps facing each other: Ramaphosa, who, in contrast to the previous conference at Nasrec in 2017, was rumoured to hold a clear majority, and the RET faction, which had hardened around its chief patron, the former health minister Zweli Mkhize, whom Ramaphosa had fired in 2021 following Special Investigating Unit (SIU) evidence of Mkhize's involvement in corruption. In this unnerving showdown, voting delegates faced a stark choice: annihilate or be annihilated.

FOR THE RET, CONTROL of the party meant control of government, the state and, therefore, its resources. It was classic oligarchic capitalism – the romance between money and power. By 2022, many key offenders in top leadership positions had been hauled before the ANC disciplinary committee and suspended. In their estimation, the run-up to the conference now called for swift and maximum exploitation. To understand the RET's modus operandi, it is necessary to understand the faction's motives, succinctly articulated by Wits University sociologist Roger Southall:

> The motive behind the faction seems to be black economic empowerment, but not the empowerment originally envisaged by Thabo Mbeki with its carefully regulated industrial charters and targets. The RET version was a generalised insistence that the state machinery (government departments, provincial and local administrations, and state-owned enterprises) be leveraged to allocate contracts to black businesses. This is justified by attacks upon "white monopoly capital", arguing that the South African economy has changed very little since democracy in 1994, and that white business is covertly determined upon maintaining white power … [Thus] the RET faction is a strong supporter of state enterprises. Although the faction would not object to the transfer of state enterprises into black hands, privatisation is feared as likely to result in acquisition of state businesses by white companies. In any case, the RET faction is heavily embedded within the

state-owned enterprises. Their operatives allocate valuable contracts to black "tenderpreneurs" – businesspeople who feed on government contracts.[34]

By implication, motives such as these would have a momentous effect on the faction's ability to award tenders to its operatives. For influential leaders of the RET who now found themselves outside the party and the state, all versions of "structural reform" touted by the Ramaphosa government and government lobbies attached to "big business" were heresy.[35] And they equated these structural reforms with fundamental departures from the ANC's founding principles and vision.

For the vast majority of RET supporters, then, their very survival depended on weakening the Ramaphosa slate at conference. And that meant manipulating the list of delegates to influence the outcome of the leadership elections. This dynamic had first played out at Polokwane, where rumours were rife of branch and provincial lists either being purged of Mbeki supporters or of delegates being persuaded by gifts of money to vote for Zuma. To the untutored, ANC conferences get under way very soon after the accreditation of branch and provincial delegates has been completed. The whole fate of conferences, in other words, lies largely in the compilation of candidate lists before conferences begin. And so a large part of the battle for leadership is won or lost in the party's branch and provincial structures ahead of conferences themselves.

As the reins of control were tightened under the Zuma faction after Polokwane, opportunities emerged to manipulate not just which leadership candidates delegates decided on, but also who attended conferences. For the most cunning operators in the party, it was an incredible opportunity. It heralded a new era of abuse by senior party leaders with access to some of the major switch points in Luthuli House. The opportunity was especially strong for those who already had a hand in the day-to-day running of the organisation. A whole brood of schemes was hatched, from blocking delegates to replacing registered names with unregistered ones; the key factor was access to the levers of power.

Within this environment, the ANC's Office of the Secretary General, tasked with running the organisation's structures, had enormous powers to influence outcomes, and it was clear to me that it had become a fiefdom for some in the RET who used it to vet or block delegates. It was in this tempestuous atmosphere that I found myself in the crosshairs of backroom manoeuvres by RET proponents.

My battle began when I tried to get accredited to attend the policy conference, which is usually held six months before the leadership conference. The policy conference deals with policy matters and reviews the various policy positions and resolutions that were taken at the previous elective conference in preparation for the upcoming one. Based on a careful assessment of the party's achievements and weaknesses, delegates engage in debate around policy that will guide the next five years. I almost never attend policy conferences because of my position in the resolutions committee of the elective conference. On this particular occasion, however, I decided to go to the policy conference. If I wanted to gauge which grouping was in command, the policy conference would give me a very good idea of the elective conference in six months' time.

The policy and leadership battles were make or break affairs, and rather than watch the drama from a distance, I wanted to hurl myself into the thick of things, with my weight behind Ramaphosa and his policies. As far as I was concerned, Ramaphosa stood above the fray as the only guarantor of policy certainty and stability in the ANC. But I also knew that the difficulties of his first term meant that not all policies adopted in 2017 had seen the light of day. It was as if he had been in a permanent state of war to dismantle the apparatus of state capture. I felt that perpetual crises meant that, beyond the national obsession with the leadership contest, some of the most sensitive policy issues had not been settled.

The conference came and went, and I was satisfied with the overall direction. The challenge centred mainly around implementation and capacity in the ANC and government. Shortly after the conference, I found myself, very publicly, and not without scathing criticism from the RET, putting my loyalties at the service of Cyril Ramaphosa's cause in regular columns that were widely read. I had never met Ramaphosa personally, but I liked him as a candidate to lead the country. I felt that his vision for South Africa steered the ANC and government away from the madness of the Zuma government's smash-and-grab policies towards the glorious times when the ANC actively championed the principles and goals of non-racialism, non-sexism, equality, prosperity and social cohesion.

In the intensifying relationship between state resources and power that had become the hallmark of the Zuma oligarchy, I saw Ramaphosa's presidency as a decisive turning point. From the outset, he presented himself as an economic reformer and launched new plans to reconstruct the economy. He declared that his goal was to vanquish state capture, reset the economy on a new growth path that would be generative of greater investment flows, and help restore a model of Black Economic Empowerment (BEE) that he himself had helped design when he chaired the BEE Commission, established by President Thabo Mbeki in the early 2000s.

I remember my own first impressions of Ramaphosa's 2019 State of the Nation (Sona) speech: a sensible vision and policy framework that had all the ingredients of a turnaround plan. The stakes were enormous and real: the state was hollowed out and many of the culprits responsible for looting its resource were on the loose. The whole fate of the country as an investor-friendly economy lay in whether policies and institutions could be stabilised.

And here it is important to see that Ramaphosa was not advocating a sudden leap to a free market. His enthusiasm for a private sector-led growth path was finely balanced against the role of the state in containing the vagaries of the market and correcting historical imbalances, thus ensuring that those on the margins of the economy were taken care of. While his most important act was to break the stranglehold of corrupt individuals on the state, he had in mind not the transfer of state wealth into private hands, but the creation of a developmental state built on strong institutions and capable individuals.

During a time in South Africa of widening inequalities, growing poverty, unrestrained financial institutions and perpetual crises, my sense was that Ramaphosa's advocacy of state regulation and strong institutions was as important as economic stabilisation and liberalisation. His overarching concern and long-term vision was the creation of conditions for a massive spurt in foreign direct investment.

Against the backdrop of a contracting economy, business closures and job losses, he introduced his Economic Reconstruction and Recovery Plan in October 2020, setting out his vision and priorities. Addressing a joint sitting of parliament on 15 October that year, he detailed extraordinary measures, including "aggressive infrastructure investment and employment programmes to create jobs, the reindustrialisation of the economy, the acceleration of reforms to unlock investment and growth, combatting corruption and sharpening the capabilities of the state".[36]

It was an ambitious agenda, and one I fully embraced in my columns. But my public stance was to create enduring problems for me; problems that would culminate in the difficulties I experienced in the build-up to the December 2022 conference. That I spoke truth to power in my columns only made me a greater target, as did my previous book on the post-Zuma era, which positioned me firmly behind Ramaphosa and exposed a great deal of the ambition and corruption in the party.

WHEN, AFTER THE POLICY conference, I struggled to get accredited as part of the drafting committee, my suspicions were fuelled by intelligence relayed to me by my own sources in the ANC that it was one of the acting deputy secretary generals at Luthuli House, after the untimely death of Jessie Duarte, which gave her considerable power over the organisational and logistical work that went into preparing for the conference. It was an open secret that she was in the RET camp.

The information my intelligence sources came out with was remarkably accurate. The person concerned, they told me, had gone out of her way to block my attendance, first at the policy conference and then the upcoming December conference. When my comrades tried to get me accredited as part of the conference bureaucracy, charged with managing back-end conference proceedings, she flatly refused. Then they suggested inviting me as a service provider who had done work within the ANC and who they valued. Once again, she refused. Finally, they tried putting me on the guest list as an academic, and thus part of a list of civil society representatives that routinely get invited to conferences. That avenue, too, was rejected.

If it was a clear warning shot for me, I decided I was not going to despair. That would play into the plan to frustrate me and, eventually, get me to back off. Determined to outmanoeuvre her, I moved with great haste to put certain counter-measures in place in time for the conference. If my intelligence was correct, and I had no reason to doubt it, I was convinced that the only route to the conference was to circumnavigate the problem.

It was sometime in August that I accepted an invitation from the ANC Veterans League president Snuki Zikalala to join the drafting team of the arts, culture and archives subcommittee. It was not something I wished, but it was my Plan B: a stealthy back-door entry into conference when all other avenues were closed. As December approached, I felt my chances of getting on to the drafting committee were waning. I knew that, ordinarily, Spongy Moodley would invite team members to a meeting at Luthuli House well ahead of the conference. With a few days to go before conference, that seemed unlikely.

And so it was on that December afternoon, as I sat down to lunch, that I experienced a release when, five months after the policy conference and my first faltering steps to get accredited, I received Moodley's WhatsApp message instructing all drafting team members to report to a venue near the Nasrec Expo Centre south of Johannesburg. But this time round, there were conditions attached to joining the committee. One requirement was that committee members were to refrain from writing media columns or talking to journalists during the conference. I suspected this was a direct result of my columns and my second book. I knew already that there were a significant number of senior leaders in the ANC who felt my approach in my book was too sceptical. As I have mentioned, some saw it as washing the party's dirty linen in public, something that has been a taboo in the ANC since its exile years when conferences were held in secrecy to avoid attracting the attention of the apartheid regime and Western intelligence.

I agreed to the conditions and heaved a sigh of relief.

ON WEDNESDAY MORNING, a day before the start of the conference, I got into my car and took the M2 South motorway. My first stop was in Rosebank, where I picked up my friend and comrade Michael Sachs. Then we proceeded to Crown Mines, a suburb not far from the conference venue.

When, at 10 am, we eventually arrived to find a throng of delegates surrounded by security detail, reality set in. The mere fact that we had made it there seemed like a minor victory. One of the more articulate expressions of the mood came from a comrade on the drafting team: "Presidentialising the ANC starts at these gates to conference," he told me. "It depends which side of the gate you're on," I replied. Little did we then know that though we had finally made it to the conference venue, we were still on the other side of the gate. And then began the wait.

WHILE THERE WAS A clear protocol behind the tight security, there were subterranean currents at work, too. We were to feel the first tangible effects of this as voting delegates arrived and were shuttled through security after rigorous searches and identity checks. Unlike others, we could not access the venue. When we asked the security officers what the problem was, we were told that there were "security glitches" that had to be resolved because the system could not confirm our membership. "How is that possible when other delegates were allowed in?" one comrade in our team asked.

"It's the system. If it says you can't enter, you will not enter," the guard replied.

An hour turned to five hours as we waited outside the entrance to the venue amidst a group of comrades toyi-toyiing and singing as they made their way to the security checkpoint. By this time, we had every reason to be wary. It was one thing waiting for a minor security glitch to be resolved; it was quite another, however, waiting five hours under a flaming ball of sun without word from anyone. No matter, we thought, we were members of the drafting team. There was simply no way we would not be allowed in. At 5 pm, we received a WhatsApp message from Moodley apologising for the technical glitch and instructing us to return to the venue the following morning.

I drove home that evening, physically tired and exasperated, trying to understand whether I had been the reason for the delay. We had, after all, been members of the drafting team since 1996. If this was a five-hour glitch, why, then, were other delegates allowed into the venue and not us? Perhaps I was disappointed, too, because we had lost a day of preparations in the drafting team and of spirited celebrations with our comrades inside the venue ahead of the start of conference.

Then it dawned on me that evening: the sense of disappointment I felt was not so much because of thwarted expectations or physical fatigue from the five-hour wait, but, more profoundly, because I found myself in the crosshairs of a factional showdown in the ANC. I felt excluded, on the outer edges of the conference. With that thought swirling in my mind, I got an early night's sleep.

EARLY ON THURSDAY morning I got into my car and headed back to the registration venue. I arrived at the security check and met other members of the team, among them Kenneth Creamer, Michael Sachs, Febe Potgieter, David Makhura and a number of director generals. Delighted to be allowed through the gates, we then were confronted with yet another delay: we could not proceed to the conference venue without our accreditation lanyards. More worrisome was the problem this time: two machines mysteriously could not print the lanyards when all around us delegates were being handed theirs. The lanyards are straightforward laminated access cards bearing a picture and designation of the conference attendee. It also designated whether you are a voting or non-voting delegate and, therefore, whether you had restricted access, in the case of the media and guests, or full access to the conference, in the case of delegates. My position on the drafting team meant that I was a non-voting delegate.

The security officials in charge of processing the lanyards were dour and earnest. In fairness, they did not decide who got access cards; they followed instructions and sometimes found themselves at the mercy of faulty machines. But this was no technical glitch again. It was a day before the start of conference, and here we were in a two-day misadventure to get something as simple as lanyards. I wondered, in that moment, as did many of my comrades on the drafting team, why our security approval did not automatically entitle us to lanyards.

Perhaps it was a measure of the ANC's bureaucratic ineptitude that there was such administrative chaos. For an activist in the ANC, walking into an administrative roadblock at the highest decision-making gathering of the party had a sadly enervating effect. That sense of exclusion I had felt when I arrived home the previous evening returned. What is it that engenders such inefficiency? I wondered. Perhaps it was a deliberate intention, perfectly choreographed since the previous day, to block our entry.

MINUTES TURNED TO HOURS, and by the end of the day we had not been given our lanyards. Together with our status as non-voting delegates was an unstated view that we were not priority cases in the administration of security checks and registration. Intellectually, I understood and supported this. It was important to get voting delegates into the venue in time for the conference. But a two-day wait was unacceptable. Irritated, we demanded to know what was going on. When we tried again to find out why the administrative officials were not running a parallel system for voting and non-voting delegates, stressing all the while that time was running out, we were met with blank stares.

By the late afternoon the team sat under the cover of a tree, waiting. Eventually, senior ANC leaders started trickling in. Among them were Paul Mashatile and Gwen Ramokgopa. They had received reports that things were not moving fast enough, certainly not fast enough to meet the starting gun to the conference the next morning. When Ramokgopa spotted some of us under the tree, she immediately headed towards us. Seeing this as our only solution, we complained bitterly about the two-day wait, the long-winded and stultifying process of dealing with the administrative process of registering delegates, and our frustration and disappointment at not being able to get our lanyards. Ramokgopa took it upon herself to sort out the problem.

In little less than an hour we were asked to report to the registration table. There, nicely displayed, were our lanyards. They had been there, in a box, all along. By this time, I had no doubt in my mind that it was a delaying tactic to frustrate some of us.

When, finally, we made our way to the conference venue, we passed the acting deputy secretary general who I believed was behind the delays to our accreditation. "Why didn't you come to me earlier?" she asked. "You should have told me you were waiting. I would have sorted you out long ago." It was a provocative statement, one we chose to ignore. We had our lanyards. We were in, and that was all that mattered.

Fortunately, by the time we entered the conference hall the proceedings had not started. It is not an overstatement to say that the first two days were a monumental disaster, so much so that the entire conference was delayed by a day and a half because of the ineptitude of certain administrators and the bureaucratic shenanigans of political office-bearers. There was talk at the conference of certain delegates, who had confirmed their attendance, being removed from the list in order to make way for other delegates, obviously aligned to the RET faction. There were even incidents, reported to the conference organisers, where branch delegates arrived only to find that they had been replaced by other delegates. It was a stark reminder of the lengths to which RET factionalists were prepared to go to influence the outcome of the elections. One can only imagine the chaos in the administration of over 4,000 delegates who had to be accredited, seated and fed. The first two days were, without exaggeration, a nightmare.

Inside the conference venue, the walls of the plenary hall were festooned in black, green and gold – the signature colours of the ANC. As I entered, a handful of delegates were milling around the middle of the hall, talking in hushed tones. In that still moment, the free-floating state of rivalry and public rancour outside the walls of the room disappeared. I felt enormous pride in this large organisation with an even larger history. Here, within four walls, was the heart of the ANC laid bare, under whose banner successive generations have marched since 1912.

The size of this history has not been fully appreciated by the ANC's detractors, who prefer tainting the organisation with the corruption of a generation whom Kgalema Motlanthe once described as "alien tendencies". As I stared at the podium in quiet contemplation, a voice rang out. My colleagues and I were being directed through yet another security check for support staff. Three other checkpoints were for voting delegates from all branches and provinces. I headed to a room at the back of the hall that had been made available for our team. Some of my comrades, whom I had not seen in years, were already seated. We greeted each other and made small talk about family and work, and then waited.

When conference finally started, I made my way to the floor of the gathering. In the heady onrush of the opening, delegates broke out into jubilant song and dance. For a moment, it looked like a glorious movement, united by a vision emblazoned in the party's colours. A sense of unreality, at once exhilarating and tense, filled the air. Against this, however, were ranged the antagonisms and factional divisions that had first surfaced in 2007 when Mbeki was removed. It was noticeable from the floor that delegates brought to the conference the deep fractures in the ANC that had sundered the party into rival factions. In the chaos of the Zuma years, those divisions deepened as the state seemed to tear itself apart.

Characteristically, the songs that were sung, which are prepared and rehearsed by delegates months before the conference, reflected rival support for the two main candidates for the presidency, Cyril Ramaphosa and the RET's chief patron, Zweli Mkhize. It was clear to me that the Mkhize camp was spearheaded by an essentially KZN slate, reflected in placards delegates were brandishing. But unlike the previous conference, where Zulu regalia and songs were on full display, this time round the KZN faction was more muted, reflecting their weakness rather than their numbers. But they were not going to go down without a fight.

A few minutes later, ANC chair Gwede Mantashe stepped up to the podium and instructed delegates to settle down for the president's arrival. When Ramaphosa entered the hall, the floor erupted into even louder song and dance. The theme song was about Ramaphosa and the R350 Covid grant he had allocated to those in need. But even here, at a seminal moment when the president provides a comprehensive statement of the state of the nation, the shenanigans of the RET were on full display. As delegates took their seats and Ramaphosa began his political report, the hall broke out into rowdy ululation. Zuma had arrived, flanked by no less than twenty bodyguards, a full twenty minutes into the president's address.

I had no doubt that the timing was deliberately intended to disrupt the president's political report and, instead, abruptly turn the attention of delegates to Zuma. With former president Mbeki already seated, it was a flagrant violation of conference protocol, but this was classic Zuma – a serial exhibitionist who prided himself on his mastery at stealing the limelight. Ever the avuncular diplomat, Ramaphosa stepped aside to acknowledge Zuma. What magnified the moment is that just a day before, Zuma had brought a personal prosecution against the president. Mkhize, too, was late. And, again, his backers broke into song when he arrived.

By this time Mantashe's patience was wearing thin. He stepped up to the lectern to put a stop to the spectacle. "We are not going to allow this to continue, and you are urged to take your seats," he told the room. The moment may have whipped up a sense of chaos, but unlike previous conferences the gravitational centre was Ramaphosa's ANC. The reins were not about to slip, and after a few minutes delegates sat down and Ramaphosa delivered his political report from a lectern wrapped in black, green and gold bunting. The conference theme, he said, "called upon delegates to … pursue with greater vigour the rebuilding and renewal of the ANC, and, as a united movement, to advance the fundamental transformation of our economy and society".[37]

As I watched the president carve a space for us to redeem the ANC and build on the ashes of the economic devastation of the Zuma era, I felt a sense of release. Here was a room packed with delegates whose spirits seemed energised by the collective purpose the president was invoking. Was that my fantasy? I wondered in that moment what more the RET faction had up its sleeves. Ramaphosa may have won the loyalty of a majority of the NEC leadership – and, if the voting patterns were to be believed, of most branches – but conferences were often open season for participants: from the songs sung to disruptions.

Then Ramaphosa struck a tone that was a foretaste of the day's proceedings: "We have a new membership system as directed by the 54th National Conference to combat gatekeeping and manipulation of our democratic process,"[38] he told the gathering. It was a stark rejoinder to RET voting delegates in the room. They got the message. But they did not accept it.

COMING ON THE HEELS of the report there was a pungent air of ferment in the hall. When Ramaphosa came to the end of his report, attention turned to the credentials reports. In the absence of a secretary general to deliver the report, deputy president David Mabuza was asked to step in. But RET delegates insisted that the head of the newly formed elections committee, Kgalema Motlanthe, deliver the elections report first. This was a new structure set up by the NEC to give blood and muscle to the step-aside rule, which empowered the NEC to suspend leaders with criminal records or bar them from contesting leadership positions within the ANC. It was going to be the key battleground for the RET at the conference.

The chief protagonist in the battle was suspended secretary general Ace Magashule, who had been facing corruption charges and was therefore excluded from conference. None of this was made any easier by the decision Motlanthe had taken, as chair of the elections committee, to exclude Magashule from standing for elections. I imagined at that time how the two men would have regarded each other with contempt had Magashule been in the room.

Over the next five hours, following Motlanthe's delivery of his report, a long, endless stream of young RET delegates took to the podium to raise baseless points of order and objections. It was an orchestrated showpiece, stage-managed by RET backer Andile Lungisa, who had been suspended from the party for assaulting an opposition party MEC in the Eastern Cape. In their attempt to goad the conference into allowing Magashule, Lungisa and several other suspended RET members to stand for elections, they argued that Lungisa had paid an admission of guilt fine and that, to our surprise, Tony Yengeni, who had been found guilty of corruption in the arms deal and served jail time, had had his criminal record expunged by Zuma.

It was a puerile provocation and, as far as I was concerned, a deliberate attempt to disrupt and collapse the conference. We were already running a day late. With further delays it would have been impossible to proceed without massive logistical and financial implications.

The penny dropped when a delegate whispered in Motlanthe's ear, proposing a bold move to end the fiasco. The proposal, as we will see in the next chapter, was audacious but brilliant.

Four

Monkey business

From the moment he was suspended from the ANC in May 2021 after refusing to step aside over corruption charges, former party secretary general Ace Magashule declared publicly, and not without hubris, that his ambition was to step back into the party and its national leadership. He would often gleefully declare from that point onward that he remained a loyal cadre of the ANC. It was a desperate effort to rally support and prise open the door to the ANC NEC. Now he began to think about new horizons.

It was a sunny Friday morning, the first day of registration at the Nasrec Expo Centre, and Magashule cut a lonely figure outside the conference perimeters. As I walked towards the entrance to the venue, I passed a knot of reporters who were already badgering him about whether he wanted to be nominated from the conference floor for president, to which he declared pointedly that he might have been exiled from the party's inner sanctums, but he "was around" and electable.[39] He was imploring passing delegates to fight his suspension so that he could be part of the conference. Later that day the media ran the story with a picture of Magashule. It portrayed the man, in a bit of showmanship, brandishing a sign on the concrete floor outside Nasrec, emblematic of a large name tag, saying, "I'm here."[40]

Is the Party Over?

It was a daring thought, but there was just one problem. Unlike the 54th conference at Nasrec, when RET delegates could claim a strong presence, Magashule was outside the party, along with members of the RET faction, looking in. His rise and fall is not just a story about his own ambitions and blatant mixture of power and money. Since the Zuma presidency, state capture had become a clannish system of looting. It was giving birth to ethnic elites that were in fact factions tied to state assets, often allied to powerful party and government leaders in the RET faction. Next to Jacob Zuma, Magashule had become the most senior emblem of this cancer in the ANC.

No sooner had Zuma's been ousted from the NEC and presidency than the RET faction began angling for a return to power. Just two years earlier, in June 2021, Zuma's acolytes in the RET had staged a violent showdown in what looked like an orchestrated campaign of looting and sabotage across the country. Much of this has been well documented and does not merit attention here. Now, at the 55th elective conference, they were exiled from the centre of power, without a voice and restless. I knew that they were not going to go down without one last stand and was appalled at Magashule's showmanship. It didn't matter. On that day, I knew the real battle would be inside the perimeters of Nasrec, not outside.

It was a tense day for the Ramaphosa camp. In the desultory build-up to the first day, there was talk of candidates attempting to bribe their way to power, hints of delegates using the election process as a battleground for their comeback. And so it was with a heavy heart that I shared the anxiety of some of my comrades in the Ramaphosa camp that the electoral process was likely to become a last-ditch tool to disrupt, and maybe even shut down, the conference as their strategic gambit to pre-empt Ramaphosa's election and mobilise popular support. I was reminded at this point of one of former Russian president Boris Yeltsin's interviews with a newspaper ahead of his re-election in the early 1990s: "When a rival loses support and confidence … you must expect that he will attempt to stir up things," Yeltsin said.

WOULD THE SAME THING happen at Nasrec? It was a worrying prospect, but one that had begun to take shape over the preceding months.

There were already rumours of failed attempts to influence branch and provincial elections through pay-offs and other hidden campaign activities. My own impressions were reinforced by the details I already knew, as a participant in all party conferences since 1996, of electoral manipulations in branches and provinces since Thabo Mbeki's removal at Polokwane in 2007. The details, of course, were always secret, hidden in car boots full of black bags and brown paper envelopes exchanging hands in parking lots.

It may always be difficult to control the exchange of money, but we should not ignore the importance of branches in the leadership election process. Because of their enormous influence over electoral outcomes, branches have been the real loci of power in the ANC, the centres of grassroots articulations of policy and national leadership choices. Thus, branches earn their legitimacy in the ANC from their power to choose their national leadership candidates; a power based on rigorous discussion of policy matters and resolutions. In theory, it is a robust process, not just, as is generally assumed, a headlong battle for power. When branches eventually conclude their discussions, their choice of candidates, elected by a majority vote of 50 plus one per cent, ought to be the outcome of a careful assessment of who is best placed to champion the ANC's policies for the next five years.

In its original formulation, branch resolutions were taken to the national conference by delegates whose numbers were proportionate to the size of the branch. Thus, for every 100 members who constitute a basic branch of the ANC, that branch was entitled to one delegate to the conference. If a branch had 3,000 members, it was technically entitled to 30 members at the conference. But over the years the ANC has sought to counterbalance over-representation because of the size of certain branches within the provinces and, more recently, their correspondence to factional interests, by coming up with an equitable formula. In this formula, large branches are entitled to a fixed number of delegates.

By the time of the 55th conference, it was widely believed that the Ramaphosa slate held the balance of power in branch and provincial structures of the party. But Ramaphosa's RET opponents had other plans. Their expectations of disrupting the conference, and perhaps shutting it down, were high. But the boldness of this plan had not been fully fathomed by Ramaphosa supporters who had expected a reasonably smooth day. Inside the perimeters of conference, a little-understood gambit was a provision in the ANC's rulebook that allowed delegates to contest from the floor of conference, notwithstanding their own branch resolutions on candidates. It was a glaring loophole, but one that gave delegates every opportunity to vote after their heart's desire at the conference itself. It was a symbol of the ANC's rich culture of democracy.

WITHIN THIS ENVIRONMENT, the ANC elections committee ruled, its stewardship guided by the esteemed former president Kgalema Motlanthe. It is important to note here that the committee had never existed before, but because of the controversial 'step-aside rule', the NEC decided in the run-up to the 2022 national conference to establish such a committee. Not only would the committee set the rules and criteria for elections, but it would also be an instrument for upholding the principles of ethical leadership articulated in the ANC's famous policy paper, *Through the Eye of the Needle.*

Motlanthe was a smart choice for chairing the elections committee. With his relative neutrality and exposure to worker democracy, accountability and transparency in Cosatu, where he cut his teeth during the 1980s, combined with his impressive organisational profile in the ANC since the early 1990s, he is widely regarded as an open and collegiate leader likely to instil a culture of accountability in the ANC.[41] His fierce independence and record of sometimes quite personal dissent in the ANC made him a hero to labour during the 1990s when it appeared it wasn't winning all the time. Unofficially, he emerged untainted from the Polokwane battle, with party activists who attended the conference admiring of his apparently empathetic stance regarding social and economic issues.

To his credit, when he was appointed to chair the elections committee he set out to bring the same neutrality and transparency to the nominations process at the 55th conference. In the preceding months he assiduously put in place systems and processes outlining how the nominations process would happen, from branch and provincial nominations prior to conference to checks and balances whereby Regional Executive Committees deployed audit teams to branches to verify whether they qualified as duly constituted structures of the ANC. Those audits were rigorous, designed to determine whether there was open and fair discussion by branch members and whether resolutions on policy and leadership candidates were the outcome of discussion rather than coercion and bribery. The process was thorough, right down to minutes of discussions and nominations of leaders.

When, in late August, Motlanthe presented his proposal for new criteria for internal ANC election processes to a special NEC meeting ahead of the party's conference, it provoked a sharp backlash from the RET faction. Of particular concern to them was Motlanthe's suggestion that the new election process involved shortlisting three candidates in each position during the branch and provincial nominations as a means to vet candidates and ensure they had the capacity, integrity and support needed to lead the party. Dismissing the new rules as a violation of the ANC constitution, they questioned the fairness of those invested with power to vet candidates and decide who qualified and was disqualified from electoral processes.[42]

In truth, their protestations vividly demonstrated the clandestine streams through which so much of the RET's power had coursed: buying votes, blocking delegates, stymying debate, manipulating the rules of the game. Other NEC members, however, decided that the best way to deal with corruption was to dam up these streams. Against the chorus of opposition, the NEC decided to adopt the new rules. Motlanthe now had a mandate to deliver his elections committee report to the national conference.

IN A PACKED CONFERENCE auditorium at the start of the first day, the spotlight fell, not on Ramaphosa, but on Motlanthe. As a rule, leadership elections cannot proceed unless the credentials of all voting delegates are vetted by the branches, provinces and regions of the party, and candidacies for leadership positions are confirmed to ensure that there is no foul play. Even non-voting delegates and guests are thoroughly vetted to monitor not only who votes but who participates in closed conference sessions, where delegates often discuss internal party matters such as the state of the ANC's financial affairs.

But there is another important aspect of the credentials process that had implications for the conference: unless the credentials report is adopted, conference cannot proceed nor can the 86-member NEC be dissolved and a steering committee appointed as the de facto decision-making authority of the conference to oversee the election of a new NEC. It can be reasonably argued that, without agreement on credentials, the conference could collapse.

When Ramaphosa said in his political report that manipulation had to be countered, he may have unwittingly opened the way for reprisals. Although the committee rulebook for branch and provincial candidates was ironclad, there was a loophole in the rules for the national conference: even though branches may have transparently and fairly discussed and agreed on their leadership choices, there was always the possibility of influencing from the floor of the actual conference.

And it is here, I think, in the rough and tumble of deal-making and power-broking that voting delegates became targets of bribes by operators doing the bidding of their patrons. The fortunes of the RET in the leadership race would depend to a significant extent on corrupt machines and shady handlers. It was well known from previous conferences that RET candidates had their own unscrupulous moneymen. And when it came to stealing votes, there were always attempts to replace elected delegates with unelected ones.

In fact, there was again talk of back-alley deals, where money in brown paper envelopes exchanged hands in an attempt by the RET to influence voting outcomes. So much so that it was rumoured that Zweli Mkhize himself at some point was making use of the conference toilets to dish out money to get delegates to vote in a particular way. Whether the rumour is true or not is beside the point. What matters is that deal-making and voter manipulation were rife.

Amendments to the credentials process at the 54th conference and the creation of a credentials committee were intended to close the loophole. When Motlanthe presented his report to the conference, there was an expectation, judging from opposition at the August Special NEC, that there would be resistance and disruptions. If delegates were free in the fluid conditions of the conference to change their minds about their leadership choices, then Motlanthe insisted on two conditions. Firstly, that steps were taken to curb the culture of bribery that began in 2007 at the Polokwane conference when Mbeki was ousted. And here is it important to understand that Polokwane was the first time, in a material way, that we became aware of large sums of money playing a role in influencing the outcome of conferences. After Polokwane, the NEC realised that there was simply no way of stopping money exchanging hands outside voting booths, but there was one way of encouraging delegates to cast their votes without fear or favour. No delegate was allowed to take a cell phone or electronic device into a voting booth. It was a clever way of eliminating, not the incentive to accept money by delegates, but the proof moneymen needed that delegates voted according to the wishes of their handlers. Of course, there was no way of knowing either way. There was certainly no way of knowing whether branch delegates who arrived at the conference on a branch slate would vote according to the branch position. Cutting off proof of voting from the briber–bribee equation, as a procedural measure, was a brilliant step.

The second condition laid down by the August Special NEC and articulated by Motlanthe in his report to the conference was the step-aside rule. The 54th national conference resolved that leaders charged with corruption or other serious crimes would have to voluntarily step aside from participation in party and government activities, or face suspension. The rule followed a string of corruption cases involving high-profile party officials since 2020 who were now excluded from the 55th conference. And it would become a bone of contention well into the evening that came close to collapsing the conference. To appreciate the weight of the problem that had been thumping at the door of the 55th conference, it is necessary to first trace the origins of the step-aside rule.

AT THE HEIGHT OF the Covid-19 pandemic, in August 2020, the weekend *Sunday Independent* newspaper broke the story of Ramaphosa's spokesperson Khusela Diko and her husband amaBhaca king

Madzikane II Thandisizwe Diko being awarded tenders to the tune of R125 million by the Gauteng Department of Health to supply personal protective equipment.

Ramaphosa hauled Diko before an ANC disciplinary committee and put her on special leave pending the outcome of a full inquiry after signing a proclamation that allowed the Special Investigating Unit to probe corruption around Covid-19 social relief funds. Ramaphosa was scathing in a letter to his comrades shortly after the Diko scandal:

> The ANC and its leaders stand accused of corruption. The ANC may not stand alone in the dock, but it does stand as Accused No. 1. This is the stark reality that we must now confront. At its last meeting, at the beginning of this month, the ANC national executive committee (NEC) recognised the justifiable public outrage caused by recent reports of corruption. It is said that these developments cause us collectively to dip our heads in shame and to humble ourselves before the people.[43]

That the scandal broke right under Ramaphosa's nose, with his spokesperson the chief protagonist, must have infuriated him. In the same month, the NEC adopted Ramaphosa's sharp letter. To be sure, the proposal for a step-aside rule had already been proposed at the 2017 conference, but moves towards its implementation were sluggish until corruption in the procurement of protective equipment during the pandemic became a public outcry.[44]

Then, in October 2020, ANC secretary general Ace Magashule, who was widely touted as a prime RET presidential candidate for the 2022 conference, was arrested and charged with 21 counts – later increased to 74 – of corruption, money laundering and fraud amounting to R255 million. This related to a 2014 contract the Free State Department of Human Settlements awarded to the Blackhead Consulting joint venture (JV) to audit and remove asbestos from people's homes. Blackhead subcontracted the work multiple times, and of the R230 million paid, only R21 million ended up with the company that performed the work; as a result many Free State residents still live in homes with asbestos.[45] Magashule was suspended from the NEC pending the outcome of an investigation by the National Prosecuting Authority (NPA) into the matter.

In late 2021, the NPA accused Magashule of trying to delay his criminal trial in the Free State asbestos scandal, calling arguments in his application for seven declaratory orders from the court "vague" and "woefully inadequate". By this time the NPA could list payments that murdered businessman Ignatius Mpambani's company Diamond Hill, which was part of the Blackhead group, made at the request of Magashule's personal assistant Moroadi Cholota. She said Mpambani had paid R470,000 for tablets from a company called M-TAG Systems, another R300,000 for tablets for Cuban students, R250,000 for a delegation to visit Cuba, and R50,000 for school fees for Gupta associate Refiloe Mokoena's daughter.[46] "It is worth noting that each payment as aforementioned followed shortly after the Blackhead Consulting JV received a payment from the Free State Department of Human Settlements purportedly due in connection with the asbestos contract," the NPA said in a statement at the time.[47]

When Magashule was charged in November 2020, he said his trial was a politically motivated "fishing expedition" aimed at discrediting him and sidelining him from the ANC. Given his prominence in the NEC, he had since become the most prominent target of the step-aside rule, and as a result the NEC mandated its Top 6 party leaders, led by Motlanthe, to develop guidelines to put in place the step-aside resolution.[48]

Charged with overseeing the rule in the newly created conference elections committee, Motlanthe now faced his second test: the attempt by disgraced party leaders such as Magashule, and Andile Lungisa to elbow their way into the conference as leadership candidates nominated from the floor.

RULES, WE HAVE TO remember, can do no more than regulate behaviour. They do not necessarily mean that they are followed by all delegates. The ANC national conference itself is a roughly contested affair. In December 2022, I suspected that the elections committee would become a battleground. The moment delegates entered the conference auditorium, the RET moved into gear. When it became clear that their prime candidates would not be allowed into the conference, they began shifting the focus from voting to a sprawling and futile discussion about procedure. Their focus was clearly on mobilising support from the floor to vote against branch decisions on leadership candidates. It was a smart strategy that touched off a storm for the better part of the day's proceedings.

With the rules clarified, what happened next can only be described as an attempt to disrupt and collapse the conference. The matter had come down to the status of nominees with criminal records.

When it came to announcing the nominated candidates, delegates waited with bated breath. Motlanthe told the gathering that RET candidate Tony Yengeni, who had served jail-time for his involvement in corruption during the arms deal, did not qualify because of his criminal record. The Eastern Cape's Andile Lungisa, who had been charged with assault, also did not qualify. Their failure to make the list was squarely in line with the framework and criteria that had been agreed upon by the NEC. The decisions were not the arbitrary whims of Motlanthe.

But because of his stewardship of the elections process, Motlanthe became a target for opprobrium at the conference. RET delegates had been indoctrinated with a message of betrayal. They had come to the conference primed to oppose and disrupt Motlanthe's stewardship of the elections committee, arguing that he was at the centre of those wanting to determine who became a leader of the ANC. Of course, this was an utterly baseless allegation since it was the NEC that requested that he chair the committee and implement the criteria and framework that had been agreed on.

At some point that day, the discussion around whether RET comrades implicated in corruption like Magashule, Lungisa and Yengeni should be allowed to be nominated from the floor seemed to have deadlocked around the step-aside rule. The environment of the conference could not have been more hostile at that moment. An army of young RET backers were on their feet, demanding the mike, raising points of order and demanding clarification around the issue of the sentencing period and status of RET candidates. They argued that Magashule had a right to question his suspension and appeal to the highest decision-making organ of the ANC.

We knew that unless the matter was resolved, the credentials of delegates and candidates could not be agreed upon. And because there was always the risk at the back of our minds that endless discussion would bog us down and collapse the conference, we had to think on our feet. To put this in perspective, discussion on the status of Andile Lungisa alone lasted four long hours.

By the end of the afternoon, we were still bogged down in a circular discussion on the elections committee rules; we had not made headway towards discussing the credentials report. Amid the chaos and confusion, it felt for a while that the centre was not holding for Motlanthe and the Ramaphosa camp. It underlined the limits of Motlanthe's ability to control events. We were well into the evening, and it began to feel as if the RET could, in fact, collapse the conference.

When the Ramaphosa camp met to discuss the matter, there was concern about how much control they had over the event. A recalcitrant position on the step-aside rule would be sure to result in loss of control over the process, further delays and the possible closure of conference, which is probably what the RET faction intended. There was a sense among elections committee members by this time that a prudent approach – and way out of the deadlock – was to deal with controversial candidates as part of the credentials report.

LATE THAT EVENING a suggestion, whispered to Motlanthe by a committee member and relayed to me by the delegate, was that if the RET wanted to change the criteria and rules of the elections committee, the conference, as the highest decision-making body in the ANC, had the power to do just that. "If conference feels we must change it, then let's not exclude anyone from the elections list," the delegate told Motlanthe. "Let's agree to include them, but then they must have the required nominations from the floor."

The suggestion was risky but smart. The risk of RET candidates winning support had to be weighed against the risk of losing time and collapsing the conference. In the end there was agreement we had not been making any headway. If RET delegates were adamant about allowing controversial candidates to be nominated from the floor, it seemed sensible to allow a blanket decision by the highest decision-making body even though the previous conference had come up with rules around criminal records. The suggestion to Motlanthe made sense: let everyone be allowed to stand, provided they met the requisite minimum requirement of the percentage of the voting block to qualify.

True to his fashion, Motlanthe saw the reasonableness of the suggestion, and everyone agreed. When he eventually stood up and told delegates that he would not object to nominations from the floor for suspended party leaders, the matter was settled. It would have been easy enough to disengage rather than allow the matter to be aired. But it was, in retrospect, a clever move to allow the RET to drive their argument to its futile conclusion.

As anticipated, Magashule did not get the support he needed to stand. Andile Lungisa and others did, however, make it on to the ballot. The day's proceedings ended at 10 pm. With the RET juggernaut halted, the conference moved swiftly to discuss the credentials report. It could now also dissolve the NEC and appoint a steering committee to oversee the election of a new leadership. For the first time since conference began, I felt a sense of release.

Desperate to get some sleep, I drove home with two comrades from out of town who were sleeping over at my home. The difficult battle was won. It would be smooth sailing through the elections. I had a celebratory drink and, no sooner had I begun reflecting on the day's events than my eyelids, heavy with fatigue, closed.

Five

Unforced errors and election cock-ups

The sound and fury of the first day finally ended, but an air of nervous tension settled like a fog over the conference hall. Still smarting from their defeat over the election rules, RET delegates were, visibly, in a funk. After a fractious start to the conference on Friday, which saw Ramaphosa facing jeers, chants and calls to quit by his opponents – a ritual affair at conferences since Polokwane – it was clear to me that they were not done yet. Their presidential candidate Zweli Mkhize had come to the conference hoping to sway voters on the floor. Mkhize was the only challenger to Ramaphosa's candidacy – the other main ones, Nkosazana Dlamini-Zuma, a cabinet minister and Zuma's former wife, and tourism minister Lindiwe Sisulu, did not qualify to be on the ballot.

Mkhize had previously served as premier of KwaZulu-Natal under the Zuma government from 2009 to 2013 before stepping out of provincial politics and into the NEC of the ANC in 2012, when he was elected national treasurer general at the party's 53rd national conference. Although the front-runners in the 2017 presidential race were clearly Ramaphosa and Dlamini-Zuma, Mkhize was viewed as a possible "compromise choice", an alternative who might be viewed as electable by backers of each front-runner.

Despite Mkhize's opposition to Ramaphosa and loyalty to the RET faction at the 2017 conference, Ramaphosa appointed him minister of health in May 2019, until his removal in 2021 amid allegations that he had benefited from a state contract awarded by the Department of Health to the communications company Digital Vibes. The company was reported to have received R150 million from the department between January 2020 and February 2021 for work on campaigns for the national health insurance roll-out and Covid-19 response. Some of the costs of the Digital Vibes invoice, which included Mkhize's media appearances, appeared to have been inflated. More controversially, the company was linked to two of Mkhize's associates: Tahera Mather, his long-serving personal spokesperson, and Naadhira Mitha, a former assistant private secretary in Mkhize's ministerial office. Both had also worked as communications consultants on Mkhize's 2017 campaign for the ANC presidency. Mather and Mitha had benefited from the contracts through consultancy work for Digital Vibes.

In May 2021, the *Daily Maverick* ran explosive reports exposing Mkhize's personal connection to Digital Vibes. It was revealed that the company paid for maintenance work at a property owned by Mkhize's family trust and transferred at least R300,000 to a company owned by Mkhize's son. In early June, Ramaphosa suspended Mkhize until the latter's resignation in August that year.

Mkhize was not alone in what can only be described as an uncontrolled pandemic of corruption.

By the end of the Zuma presidency, in February 2018, the fallout of state capture left few in the RET camp unscathed – not Ace Magashule, not Mkhize and certainly not their chief patron, Jacob Zuma. And here it is important to understand what state capture had come to mean in order to understand the power dynamic behind the leadership contest at Nasrec in 2022. In concept, the RET faction had become synonymous during the Zuma years with a woolly notion that seemed to mark the end of the Mbeki era, called the "Second

Transition to Radical Socioeconomic Transformation". Despite its sweep, writes sociologist Roger Southall, the RET agenda "had no clear shape, leadership, membership, rules or policies".[49] Nor in conventional terms, according to Southall, "is the faction particularly 'radical'. The 'economic transformation' it seeks is the displacement of white racial domination, rather than the overturn of capitalism."[50]

To understand its evolution into a faction, Southall traces RET's origins to the defeat of Thabo Mbeki at the ANC's Polokwane conference in 2007 and the overlap during Zuma's nine-year presidency with state capture. "In their rhetoric, the RET argued that laying hold of the state and its resources was a sine quo non for a more radical redistribution of wealth."[51] But that was only a pretext, a carefully manufactured attempt to justify what was a blatant smash-and-grab stratagem.

If Polokwane was a turning point that eventually gave way to state capture, it did not start out that way. When, in July 2006, just days before his corruption trial, Zuma began mobilising popular support against Mbeki, with the backing of the ANC's labour allies in Cosatu and the SACP, he was not quite the rabid resource-nationalist he would soon turn out to be. Even Ramaphosa, in a clear gesture of support for Zuma around that time, did not quite see through what he described as a "team player".[52]

That Zuma commanded a coalition of disgruntled elements within the ANC-led tripartite alliance seemed to confirm a widespread conviction that a new balance of power presaged a Radical Economic Transformation agenda. To his backers against Mbeki within the ANC rank and file and its labour allies – who wanted nothing more than to tear up Mbeki's BEE legacy, genuinely confront deepening inequalities and replace that legacy with a state-driven developmental strategy – Zuma was a change agent who was likely to restore the Reconstruction and Development Programme (RDP). That kind of thinking – not out of place around that time among an emerging black business class concerned that the middle ground would soon give way – wasn't surprising in a country with such large levels of poverty and inequality.

Even Mbeki, in July 2006, a decade after GEAR's inauguration, spooled back to the principles of the RDP, citing Mandela's own call in 2002 for an "RDP of the soul".[53] On the surface, this sudden rehabilitation of the RDP may have been one of the driving forces behind the rebellion against Mbeki, but beneath the surface Zuma's ascendancy masked a more insidious agenda, the full import of which would only be grasped in later years.

Despite the disparate nature of its leaders and the vagueness of the RET agenda, the faction initially consisted of a coalition of the "walking wounded" in the tortuous build-up to Mbeki's ouster – communists, trade unionists, ethno-nationalists, resource nationalists and black economic empowerment grandees. But since Mbeki's removal and the start of Zuma's presidency in 2009, there was another, darker element at work: they had an eye on lucrative state resources. As Southall argues, "the faction drew energy from fighting against what they depicted as white domination of their professional spheres",[54] but this was nothing more than an organised smash and grab.

By the time of the ANC's conference at Mangaung in December 2012, leading RET factionalists appeared to be natural allies who shared the same populist demagoguery. If there was confusion after Mangaung about radical economic transformation, the agenda was in plain view by the time the Zondo Commission of Enquiry into State Capture began work in 2021. The South African citizenry, resentful and bewildered, now called radical economic transformation by its name: state capture.

By the time of the ANC's December 2017 national conference, the RET faction was strongly anti-Ramaphosa and pro-Nkosazana Dlamini-Zuma in the race for the ANC presidency. According to Southall, "The narrowness of Dlamini-Zuma's defeat provided it with a strong oppositional presence within the ANC during the Ramaphosa presidency, hampering his efforts at reform."[55]

THUS IT WAS, WITH Dlamini-Zuma edged out in December 2017 by a whisker and Zuma ousted in February the next year, that Zweli Mkhize arrived at the 55th conference via a scandalous route which included his active participation in provincial patronage politics in KZN and his admitted role in mobilising support for the Zuma-aligned faction, first in 2007 against Mbeki and then in 2017 against Ramaphosa. Such opposition, as we shall see, would have major implications for the 55th conference.

I knew all along, as did many other comrades, that Ramaphosa had the presidency in the bag. A lawyer by training, Ramaphosa certainly had the necessary gravitas. He may have started out an ANC outsider during the 1970s and 1980s, but he had been the firm hand behind the powerful National Union of Mineworkers (NUM) and he shot to global prominence in the early 1990s as head of the Release Mandela Committee[56] and then the behind-the-scenes power-broker at the Codesa (Convention for a Democratic South Africa) talks between the National Party and the ANC.

Although, in the early 1990s, the ANC was dominated by an exile faction, Ramaphosa's trade union background had popular appeal and he succeeded in trouncing Zuma to become ANC secretary general a year after the ANC's unbanning in 1991.[57] It was in no small measure due to his defeat of Zuma, for the second time, that Ramaphosa was now positioned as the strongest presidential candidate in 2022. He may not, this time round, have come face to face with Zuma, but his rival, Zweli Mkhize, derived his candidacy from the KZN slate.

Though Mkhize was a capable politician and public intellectual, being a medical doctor by profession, running for ANC president required a certain moral character and candour – certainly after the public outrage over state capture – and his association with Zuma and involvement in the Digital Vibes scandal had left an indelible stain on his reputation. At issue, rather, were the implications of the Mkhize-led RET faction for the powerful positions of deputy president and, perhaps, secretary general in 2022.

There was a clear logic to this. The ANC's abiding legacy, roughly since its formation, was the line of succession: if Mkhize was not strong enough to defeat Ramaphosa, then winning the deputy presidency would mean biding time until the 2028 national conference. This may not have been in Mkhize's mind, but it was certainly the motive behind the manoeuvrings that would emerge as the day progressed.

THE START OF THE day brought to the fore the factional war in the ANC in what would turn out to be a brazen attempt by the Mkhize slate to save face and at least maintain a presence in the Top 6, which by this time had been expanded to the Top 7 because of a proposal to introduce a second deputy secretary general position to take on some of the onerous responsibilities of the Secretary General's Office (SGO). Before examining the elections, it is first necessary to examine the rationale for the proposal to add a second deputy secretary general to the list. The first deputy secretary general, it had been suggested, would handle external matters such as the media, fraternal organisation and external stakeholders like the tripartite alliance partners, while the second would deal with internal ANC matters.

It was in the nature of the ANC's evolution that the size of the NEC and top leadership had adjusted to the changing operational landscape since the party's banning by the apartheid regime in 1960. What is not well known is that the total number of NEC members by the time of the landmark ANC conference in Morogoro in 1969 was only nine people, compared with its present size of eighty. To understand the small number in 1969, we must understand the conditions of illegality and need for secrecy after the party's banning.

After 1990 delegates argued that there needed to be a more expansive leadership corps to handle the weighty challenges of governing the country. Held at the University of Durban-Westville, the ANC's 1991 national conference – its first since the Kabwe conference in 1985 – was an extraordinary event described by the author Mark Gevisser in his biographical account of Thabo Mbeki as "exuberant and edgy; part American style jamboree, part struggle symposium".[58] For the first time since its banning, wrote Gevisser, "there were over 2,000 delegates – and at least that number in observers, media, diplomats and international guests".[59] The event mirrored the dramatically altered conditions under which the party would thenceforth operate. The Top 5 elders at the time meant that some accommodation had to be made for then president Oliver Tambo. Everyone knew that because Nelson Mandela was the charismatic face of the ANC, he was the first choice for president of the party. Tambo's extraordinary contribution was rewarded with the newly created position of national chairperson. And so the Top 5 became the Top 6.

Unforced errors and election cock-ups

Now we return to the elections. The expanded numbers at the 2022 conference meant greater challenges. And that, in turn, meant greater horse-trading for positions and all the slip-ups in trade-offs between rival candidates that inevitably characterise the heat of power struggles during elections.

It is no coincidence that, at the height of factional tensions over the Top 7 positions, the focus of RET delegates at the 2022 conference was not on the elections, which are unusually preceded by branch nominations before the conference, but on something less predictable: the surprise element of voting candidates from the floor of conference. In the previous chapter I discussed the loophole in the rules and the decision by the elections committee to allow all candidates, including controversial figures, to be nominated from the floor, even if this went against their branch slates.

If that was the RET strategy, they were to be bitterly disappointed. Indeed, the battle for the Top 7 was nothing short of a publicity disaster. Most unnerving of all was a series of attempts to nominate candidates from the floor who had been barred from attending the conference. And here it is important to recall that agreement had been reached on the credentials report after attempts by the RET to disrupt the conference proceedings at the start of the previous day. Consistent with the constitutional rules of the ANC, the total voting block at the conference consisted of 4,436 voting delegates, which meant that a nomination from the floor would have required 25 per cent of the total voting block by show of hands for a candidate's name to be put on the ballot paper.

Just how spontaneous was the sequence of events that followed is hard to gauge, but they would have major implications for the outcome of the elections and, potentially, the future of the country. It is necessary to understand at this point that the run-up to ANC national conferences is typically a crucial period of intense debate and lobbying for leadership candidates in branches and provinces, foreshadowing the tempo and mood of the elections at the conference. Within this intense milieu, presidential candidates square up against each other in electoral slates that broadly mark the boundary lines of contestation for the top leadership six or, in this instance, seven positions in the party's NEC.

In contrast to the 54th national conference, when the presidency contest was a neck-and-neck race between Ramaphosa and RET candidate Dlamini-Zuma, the RET's centre of gravity around Zuma, Magashule and Dlamini-Zuma was severely weakened with Zuma forced to resign, Magashule hamstrung by corruption, and Dlamini-Zuma still reeling from her defeat in 2017.

Feted by a majority in the party as the likely victor, Ramaphosa was the front-runner for the top position. More important than the question of the presidency, then, were the other two prize positions, the deputy president and secretary general. The electoral slates form the basis for what is referred to as a national caucus in the run-up to conference. The process itself is extraordinarily intense and ambitious, with teams of lobbyists for candidates for the top NEC positions criss-crossing branches and provinces across the country to rally support. By the time of the conference there is a reasonable approximation of the final list of names. However, there is no way of telling with certainty what will happen on the conference floor, where last-minute jostling and horse-trading happens.

With the hype in the hours leading to the elections around the coveted position of deputy president, who is next in line for the presidency in the ANC's succession chain, the start of the day was shrouded with suspicions in the Ramaphosa camp that there was a particular tension point around the deputy president position. Two candidates in the Ramaphosa camp had won enough support in the branches and provinces to make the list as contenders for the position. Inside the Mkhize camp was an RET faction riven by layers of difference, notably between the KZN faction and other provinces. But no matter how tightly regulated the branch nomination process was, there was no way of telling who would be nominated from the floor. Part of the dynamism of the democratic process in the ANC is the accommodation of surprise candidates. This can be relatively spontaneous and, as this conference was to demonstrate, quite disruptive and uncertain.

The first indirect blow to the Ramaphosa slate came when deputy president David Mabuza was asked whether he was available to stand for nomination to the position. Mabuza declined, saying he had given the position a great deal of thought and would not be available to serve the party and government in that capacity for another term. The blow was indirect because Mabuza was always Ramaphosa's rival and had initially emerged as an outside candidate for the presidency, with his backers in the ANC's Top 6 structure claiming "underground numbers" in numerous branches in the Free State, Limpopo and parts of Gauteng.[60]

To the untutored, Mabuza was linked to the so-called Premier League, a faction loosely aligned to the RET faction headed by Ace Magashule, with its gravitational centre in the Free State. Several ANC insiders confirmed that Mabuza had visited Zuma "cap in hand" sometime in September 2022 to seek his backing, but Zuma is alleged to have deferred to Mkhize as the RET's choice candidate for the presidency.[61] It is an open secret that Zuma never forgave Mabuza for going against his wishes in 2017 to field Dlamini-Zuma as his preferred presidential candidate. Instead, at the eleventh hour Mabuza contested on a CR17 slate for the deputy presidency in 2017.[62] It was hardly surprising, then, that when Mabuza met Zuma for the second time in September 2022, Zuma said he found it strange that candidates (like Mabuza) who wanted his backing were those who had supported Ramaphosa at the 2017 Nasrec conference.

Still, Mabuza's backers were hoping that, having failed to make the branch list, he would reach the 25 per cent threshold from the conference floor to stand against Ramaphosa for party president. Reading the floor and sensing he was on a losing ticket, he dropped out. His decision was, of course, welcomed by the Ramaphosa camp. With Mabuza out of the way, the presidency was an easy walk to victory for Ramaphosa. The outcome, though, would have unintended consequences for the Ramaphosa slate.

NEXT CAME AN AVALANCHE of strategic missteps and cock-ups that would thoroughly upend Ramaphosa's candidate for the post of deputy president. No sooner had Mabuza withdrawn than an opportunity was afforded to the floor of conference for nominees. It opened a floodgate for controversial RET-aligned individuals with criminal records, like former finance minister Malusi Gigaba (who, during Zuma's reign, was alleged to have been appointed to the finance minister position by the Gupta brothers), Andile Lungisa and many others, to enter the fray from the floor. Some did meet the minimum threshold of 25 per cent of the total conference voting block for their names to appear on the ballot; others failed dismally.

But it was Lindiwe Sisulu who, perhaps, emerged as the most dismal failure of all. With her wish to go toe to toe with Ramaphosa for the presidency, for the second time since 2017, failing to take shape, she accepted a lone call for her candidacy for the party's treasurer general position in what can only be described as a desperate, last-ditch attempt to remain in the party's top leadership. In 2017, she had settled for the deputy presidency spot at the eleventh hour, but lost to David Mabuza.[63]

Sisulu could be brash and self-serving, often preferring high drama and rowdy publicity to quiet diplomacy. She had, on more than one occasion, openly attacked Ramaphosa during the 2022 presidential race, loudly proclaiming her presidential ambitions much to the chagrin of Ramaphosa and his backers. Just months before the conference she made yet another publicity blunder by announcing her intention as tourism minister to fund an English soccer club to the tune of R1 billion at a time when the South African economy was at its lowest point since 1994. The proposal drew flak from citizens and government, and Sisulu was forced to back down from the deal.

It is hardly surprising, then, that during the branch nominations process very few delegates in the country nominated her. It was safe to assume that she did not have the backing of the Ramaphosa voting slate. Neither did she have the support of the RET camp. But Sisulu was having none of it. "People love me," she was fond of saying. But her failure was discernible in the numbers. In the end, fewer than ten hands out of a total 4,436 delegates were raised from the conference floor in support of her candidacy. It was an embarrassment, not only for Sisulu but also for the Sisulu name, which had for decades been synonymous with royalty in the ANC because of the contribution of her father and mother, Walter and Albertina Sisulu, to the anti-apartheid struggle.

At that point, I shared the concern of other comrades in the Ramaphosa camp that a worrying undercurrent of self-interest, driven by individual egos, was weakening our electoral chances for the Top 7 positions and playing into the hands of RET forces, which had managed to gain momentum in the build-up to elections later that day.

THERE WERE, BY THE late afternoon, a flurry of meetings, trade-offs and backslapping by the two caucuses in a grand chess game of tactical and strategic manoeuvres to hold the balance of power in the Top 7. The Ramaphosa camp had, however, made a costly strategic blunder in its push to take the deputy presidency. The contest between two candidates for the position in the Ramaphosa camp, justice minister Ronald Lamola and Eastern Cape premier Oscar Mabuyane, threatened to tear the caucus apart, weaken the vote and potentially hand the prize position on a silver platter to the RET.

On several occasions, leaders in the Ramaphosa camp resorted to the more direct method of trying to persuade one of the two rivals for the deputy presidency to hang back. Although, as a non-voting delegate, I was not present, I was later told by a comrade that, in the first caucus meeting at conference, Ramaphosa wanted to know whether we had the numbers to clinch the deputy presidency. In that meeting, an appeal was made to Lamola and Mabuyane not to split the votes. One of the candidates had to withdraw, with the other given the assurance that he would be accommodated in the Top 7 as treasurer general. If it was about status, there was even the promise dangled before the two of the position of national chair of the party, even though Gwede Mantashe occupied that position.

To his credit, Mantashe was magnanimous. He could see the tactical advantage that would accrue from his offer to step down from the national chair and, instead, opt for the lesser treasurer general position if it meant securing the deputy presidency for the Ramaphosa caucus. Being a seasoned cadre in the ANC, Mantashe knew that leadership was not about the actual position but the power you have as a collective in strategic leadership positions of the organisation. Being part of the Top 7, he said to the two candidates, was a massive achievement that would enable whoever stepped down from the contest to position himself to influence the party. And so, he formally offered to step aside as national chair and accept the treasurer general position. A consummate humourist, Mantashe even made light of the moment, saying, "Look at me. Do you want a treasurer general that looks like me?" – implying that with his bulk he was not exactly a model of good fiscal management. "If it is going to break the stalemate and strengthen our position, then I'm happy to be TG," he said.

But with the whiff of power under their noses, both Lamola and Mabuyane were recalcitrant. By the end of the meeting, both candidates flatly refused to back down.

AT THE SAME TIME as these events were unfolding, others outside the Ramaphosa camp waited. We had long suspected that outgoing deputy president David Mabuza's long-standing relationship with ANC treasurer general Paul Mashatile also failed to assist Mabuza in his bid for the position because Mashatile, as we will see, had allegedly used his office and that of the secretary general – which he was caretaking by this time in an acting capacity – to consolidate support for his own play for the deputy president position. Mashatile solidified support after the suspension of Magashule as secretary general in 2021 and the untimely death of deputy secretary general, Jessie Duarte.

Realising that time was running out, a second caucus meeting was called by the Ramaphosa camp, at which Ramaphosa now personally appealed to Lamola and Mabuyane to set their narrow self-interests aside. Ramaphosa said he was focused not just on the evening's elections, but on ensuring a balance of power that would enable him to course-correct the party's and country's trajectory. Then he criticised the two candidates, crisply rattling off his verdict on each. "You are the only obstacles here," he said, imploring them to "at least find it within yourselves to compromise. I'm open to either of you but you have to resolve the matter." If they could not, he said, the caucus would decide who would appear on the list for deputy president.

At some point during the caucus, the Ramaphosa slate had quietly dropped Lamola in a last-ditch effort to crack the whip. Mabuyane, they decided, would be the party's choice candidate. Mabuyane had been premier of the Eastern Cape since May 2019 and was a staunch Ramaphosa loyalist. He was previously MEC for economic development, environmental affairs and tourism in the Eastern Cape provincial government from May 2018 to May 2019. Formerly a businessman, like Ramaphosa, Mabuyane rose to political prominence through the ANC and ANC Youth League in the Eastern Cape, where he was elected ANC provincial secretary in 2009 and ANC provincial chairperson in 2017 before his translation to the Eastern Cape provincial legislature in February 2018. However, he had limited experience in national government and had also been facing allegations of corruption in the Eastern Cape.

In October 2021, Mabuyane was implicated in an investigation by Public Protector Busisiwe Mkhwebane into the alleged misuse of public funds by the Eastern Cape provincial government.[64] In 2018, the provincial government had set aside R3.3 million to host events commemorating Winnie Madikizela-Mandela. The Public Protector's investigation found that a portion of the money, R450,000, had been used to renovate the private residence of Mabuyane, who at the time was an MEC.[65] Mkhwebane referred her findings to the Hawks for criminal investigation, suggesting that Mabuyane and other officials had "improperly benefitted from the misuse of public funds" and might have contravened the Prevention of Organised Crime Act or Prevention and Combating of Corrupt Activities Act.[66] Mabuyane denied the allegation of misconduct, and suggested that the criminal investigation was unconstitutional and had been influenced by suspended ANC secretary general Ace Magashule.[67]

Lamola's case for standing his ground, however, was not over Mabuyane's tainted record. He was adamant that he had received far more votes for the position from branches and provinces – about 900, to Mabuyane's 360 votes mainly from his home province of the Eastern Cape.[68] The sensible thing, Lamola seemed to be saying, would be for Mabuyane to hang back and accept either the national chair or treasurer general position that was on offer by the caucus. But convinced he had the backing of the Ramaphosa slate – and the president himself

– Mabuyane dug his heels in. The caucus ended in a stalemate.

When, eventually, it came to election time that Sunday evening, there was a tangible sense of excitement mixed with anxiety among delegates in the auditorium. This was the moment we'd all been waiting for. It was the whole point of the conference. The rules of the election were spelled out and various provinces were told what their time slots were for casting their votes.

The divisive behaviour of Lamola and Mabuyane, who had effectively split the vote, meant that the second highest candidate would slip in. By contrast Mabuza at the previous Nasrec conference had had a very clear strategic plan. He knew that a particular segment of votes was going to carry him across the line. And by betraying his RET comrade, he dragged Ramaphosa across the line with himself as deputy president. It was a very sophisticated plan, cleverly worked out between him and Mashatile.

But in this instance, there was a complete absence of strategy and foresight by the two prime candidates in the Ramaphosa camp. Both Lamola and Mabuyane were far too concerned with their own ambitions to see the bigger picture. in the end the prize would be handed to an outside choice. This outcome, as we shall see in subsequent chapters, may yet prove to be a game-changer, with large implications for the future of the party and the country. Perhaps the most significant feature of the unfolding drama was that it may well herald an outcome, not in 2027, when the ANC's next national elective conference will be held, but as early as the next general elections in 2024.

Six
The accidental chief

The nervous build-up, through the course of Saturday, around the contest for the coveted position of deputy president found Paul Mashatile in a spot of bother. The day began, we recall from the previous chapter, with two main rivals in the Ramaphosa camp, Oscar Mabuyane and Ronald Lamola, squaring up to each other, despite attempts by leading figures in the Ramaphosa camp to persuade either of the two to step down and allow a single candidate to galvanise votes for the bigger cause. In the ensuing contest, the most ominous threats came not from outside the Ramaphosa camp but from within.

What hurt the Ramaphosa slate was not the electability of the Mkhize caucus's candidacy for deputy president but the internecine tussle between Lamola and Mabuyane. For the Ramaphosa camp, events took an ominous turn on Saturday evening when it became evident that both Mabuyane and Lamola, driven by personal egos and ambitions, were out of touch with reality.

By the early evening, the irresolute and weakened Ramaphosa slate left no one unscathed – not Mabuyane, not Lamola, not the Mkhize camp. The Ramaphosa caucus was tarnished by in-fighting. The Mkhize camp was initially none the wiser as to whether Mashatile, who saw an opportunity to mop up votes in the Ramaphosa camp, would contest the position on its list. The situation left a power vacuum in its wake. The bigger picture remained unresolved. There was no obvious successor to David Mabuza.

Such missteps meant playing hardball, and Mashatile was practised at the game. With his loyalties in neither camp, Mashatile had room for manoeuvre. No one could blame him for his ambition. His reputation was not damaged. He knew that his relative detachment from both factions gave him the tactical advantage of playing both sides. But it also carried the risk of neither side backing him. After an initial period of prevarication, the Mkhize camp by this time had openly thrown its support behind Mashatile as their preferred candidate for deputy president. They had good reason to back him. When the nominations process began on Friday afternoon, Mashatile emerged as one of the front-runners for the deputy presidency: with the Ramaphosa slate severely weakened by contestation between Mabuyane and Lamola, Mashatile had slipped in by election time on Saturday as the favoured candidate of branches in seven of the party's nine provinces, with the exception of the Eastern Cape, which favoured Mabuyane, and Mpumalanga, which favoured Lamola. But there was just one problem: by reason of his detachment from both camps, Mashatile also appeared to have a foot in both the Mkhize and Ramaphosa camps, which meant he ran the risk of losing the potential support of voters in both camps. How that came to pass is a story of his chequered rise in the ANC.

PERHAPS, IF WE ARE to identify a moment when Paul Mashatile began his ascendancy in the ANC and government, from several ministerial portfolios in the Gauteng provincial government to national leadership, it was his support for Jacob Zuma in the battle to unseat Thabo Mbeki from power at the party's Polokwane conference in December 2007. It was after Mbeki's removal that he was appointed, for the first time, to a cabinet post in Zuma's government, serving as minister of arts and culture between 2010 and 2014, an appointment that was no doubt a gesture of Zuma's gratitude for Mashatile's unequivocal support in the populous province of Gauteng.

But the onrush of events leading to the party's 53rd national conference at Mangaung in December 2012 opened a power vacuum as allegations of corruption against Zuma began to provoke an angry reaction from both citizens and some party leaders, mortified not by Zuma's candidacy but by his brazen abuse of high office. Indeed, the Polokwane SACP–Cosatu–ANC Youth League alliance behind Zuma had by this time begun to fragment. Powerful Zuma supporters such as Tokyo Sexwale, Mathews Phosa, Julius Malema, Zwelinzima Vavi and Paul Mashatile for the first time openly opposed Zuma.

It may not have been what Mashatile wanted to hear, having been instrumental in Zuma's rise, but it is what he got. What matters for this analysis is that with Mbeki out of the way and Zuma's presidency ideologically inchoate and fractured, individual candidates for leadership positions began to develop an electoral identity of their own; candidate slates, as Dirk Kotze argued around that time, began to play less of a role than in the past.[69]

By the time of the ANC's policy conference in mid-2012, a precursor to the elective conference in December, a turning point had been reached. The Gauteng ANC, and Mashatile personally, now publicly supported leadership change in the ANC ahead of Mangaung.[70] One senior NEC member in the party told me over dinner on the eve of the 55th conference elections that Mashatile, to his credit, openly challenged Zuma at an NEC meeting sometime in 2012 in preparation for the Mangaung conference. Risking his cabinet position and leadership in the party, Mashatile told Zuma that he ought to pay back the money for his Nkandla upgrades to National Treasury.

The move was seen by many NEC members sitting in that meeting as career suicide. Outwardly, Zuma might have given the impression of a convivial statesman, but within the powerful NEC of the ANC he ruled by decree. And here was Mashatile openly challenging, in a meeting of senior ANC leaders, his decision to upgrade his homestead. It was a brave and remarkable performance, the NEC member told me, at a time when most NEC members appeared to justify the upgrades to Zuma's Nkandla home, brandishing presentations of the fire pool that had been built, ostensibly to dowse flames should the thatch roof catch fire. It was a silly and transparent ruse, but, rather than fight, the few

NEC members opposed to the upgrade lost their nerve. "They threw in the towel, and it was Paul who was the first to stand up and speak his mind," the NEC member said to me.

In his version of the NEC meeting, my source recalled Mashatile telling Zuma that it was in the best interest of the ANC to pay back the money. "It is also in the best interest of all of us parliamentarians that you take the wind out of the sails of the EFF, who are using every opportunity to disrupt and create chaos, all because of these upgrades," my source recalled Mashatile telling Zuma.

But more revealing than Mashatile's valiant stand was Zuma's cunning. The NEC comrade anecdotally related Zuma's recollection at the same meeting of the famous "Chris Hani Memorandum" at the ANC's landmark Morogoro conference in 1969. "I am sharing this to show Paul's strength of character," he told me. "You see, Zuma had a tendency to talk to us as if we were children, as if he was the only seasoned senior cadre within the movement," he said, adding:

> When at that meeting Zuma said something around the "Memorandum" he claimed was prepared by Chris Hani to try and assist in the difficult conversations that were going to take place at the Morogoro conference, and Zuma made a bold statement to say that the "Memorandum" was not written by Chris Hani, comrade Pallo Jordan raised his hand and said, "You know, Mr President, this is now going to be the second time I have to correct you on historical facts because what you just said isn't true. You see, firstly, you were not at the Morogoro conference. Let's start there. Secondly, it was me, [Thabo] Mbeki and Zola Skweyiya who were asked by the [then] president comrade Oliver Tambo to go and engage with Chris around that particular issue and we spent the whole night discussing and debating with him. So I'm not sure where you get your information about that Memorandum because you were not there. We were there at that conference.

Zuma was furious but did not respond. He was skilled at choosing his moments; he would get his comeuppance. The end of the NEC meeting did not settle the most sensitive issue: what to do about Nkandla. It was in the nature of Zuma's insatiable ambition that the meeting ended with a report dripping contempt. Not only did he launch a rather garbled and vituperative attack against Mashatile's open defiance and Jordan's cheeky historical lesson, but he vehemently denied any wrongdoing with the Nkandla upgrade. It was his final say, and in the nature of NEC protocol no one could rebut it. In his presentation of the report Zuma said only that he was not going to apologise for being on Robben Island at the time of the Morogoro conference. Neither would he agree to Mashatile's request that he pay back the money for the Nkandla upgrades. It was his final word on the matter. But that was not end of his comeuppance where Jordan and Mashatile, were concerned.

Jordan paid the supreme price for his defiance. Within weeks of the NEC meeting, a leak to the media revealed that Jordan did not hold a doctoral qualification, a title he had used since his exile years. The scalding narrative that emerged in the media was just as Zuma probably intended: Jordan was publicly discredited and hung out to dry. With his reputation in tatters and his back to the wall, he resigned from public office and retreated to a solitary backbench in parliament. Sadly, for someone of his stature and role in the liberation movement, Jordan never really recovered from that blow.

A similar fate awaited Mashatile, who, according to my source, had already braced himself for trouble after the dust-up with Zuma over Nkandla at the NEC meeting.

TWO WEEKS LATER, there was one of those famous midnight cabinet reshuffles. Mashatile woke up the following morning to news that he had been shuffled out of his ministerial position. He had to return to Gauteng province to take up a lesser MEC position.

No sooner had he returned to the Gauteng provincial legislature than there were media reports that he was using his influence within the province to lobby for Zuma's removal, and possibly for his own elevation to a national leadership position at Mangaung.[71] Switching alliances at the conference, he stood for national treasurer general on a slate aligned to presidential challenger Kgalema Motlanthe. I, too, saw Motlanthe as a choice candidate against Zuma, and openly backed him.

But like Motlanthe, Mashatile lost the vote resoundingly, and Zuma backer Zweli Mkhize was appointed treasurer general by 2,988 votes to his 961.[72] He also failed to gain enough votes to win a seat on the party's Top 6 or NEC, for that matter, although he remained an *ex officio* member of the NEC in his capacity as provincial chairperson. Mkhize ran on an informal slate aligned to Zuma, who was re-elected ANC president at the conference. He was also rumoured to have been involved in recruiting the businessman Cyril Ramaphosa to run for the deputy presidency on that slate.

Soon after Mangaung, Mashatile retreated to the backbenches of the National Assembly, where he served as chair of the appropriations committee. He left the national legislature in February 2016, when he was appointed MEC for human settlements and cooperative governance in the cabinet of Gauteng premier David Makhura, a close ally, and served in the provincial cabinet until early 2018, when he took up the full-time party position of ANC treasurer general.

But Mashatile was still on his feet, all the while remaining a staunch opponent of Zuma. After the 2016 Constitutional Court judgment on Zuma's misconduct in the Nkandla saga, Mashatile spearheaded the Gauteng ANC's call for Zuma to step down ahead of the party's 54th national leadership conference at Nasrec in 2017, a call he later repeated in the week before Zuma was recalled by the ANC.[73]

At the Nasrec conference, Mashatile was elected treasurer general of the ANC. It also marked the end of Zuma's term as party president. Mashatile won 2,517 votes, against 2,178 for Maite Nkoana-Mashabane.[74] He ran on the slate of the winning presidential candidate Cyril Ramaphosa, and reportedly partnered with David Mabuza in negotiating access to that slate. Some commentators have even suggested, and not without reason, that Mashatile had a long-running and instrumental role in engineering Ramaphosa's ascent.

AND SO IT WAS THAT Mashatile arrived at the 55th conference at Nasrec with a foot in – and out of – both the Mkhize and Ramaphosa camps. Now he found himself in a double bind: not only was he out of favour with Mkhize and Zuma, but he also appeared to lack the tactical advantage of Ramaphosa's backing. We can only guess that Ramaphosa's reasoning may have had something to do with Mashatile's backing of Zuma at Polokwane and his flirtation with the RET in some of his more radical public utterances on the economy in recent years.

Paradoxically, if Mashatile's inclination to the RET faction during and immediately after Mbeki's removal from power was a factor, the same could be argued about Ramaphosa, who very publicly venerated Zuma after the Polokwane coup as a "good listener" and moderate reformer who would "steer the country into a new investment-friendly era".[75] Of course, it can be argued that in the trench warfare between the Zuma and Mbeki factions at Polokwane, a number of comrades who backed Zuma were not necessarily friends with both candidates.

As Adam Habib observed in an interview with the *Finweek* editor Malcolm Ray around that time, "A number of people in the ANC were throwing in their lot with Zuma because they felt the momentum was there: they thought Zuma was raising important questions about democracy and the economy but where some were also hoping that, with Mbeki out of the way, Zuma's corruption case (scheduled by the NPA for August 2008) would resolve the Zuma dilemma in the sense that he would no longer be a candidate for president of the country."[76]

My own impression is that Habib may have had a point: Ramaphosa's support for Zuma was not unequivocal. Neither was Mashatile's. Perhaps Mashatile instinctively felt that his chances in the Ramaphosa camp were far greater because, like Ramaphosa, he had turned against Zuma and the RET, but in politics timing is everything and this was not 2007.

In fact, by late Thursday through to early Friday, I had been interacting with comrades in the Mashatile group before the nominations later that day. They were devastated by the turn of events, telling me that they had completely lost the plot. They were not accommodated in either the Ramaphosa or Mkhize groupings precisely because Mashatile had a foot in both camps. He could not make up his mind about whom he should throw in his lot with.

Hours before the election on Saturday, he was exiled, with neither side trusting him. It seemed to me that Mashatile had made a huge mistake in devoting his energy to shadowboxing with both sides. I wrote in my notebook around that time that he could have run a strong campaign on a Ramaphosa ticket, but he never did and consequently set himself up for defeat. Was I wrong?

Politics, wrote the historian Thomas Pakenham, is an unpredictable game played with a loaded dice. Anything that can happen will happen, sometimes in a matter of minutes, sometimes hours. And lo and behold, Mashatile veered into an unexpected course of action at the eleventh hour. Just before the elections began on Saturday, I was told by some of Mashatile's backers that they had approached him and said in no uncertain terms that if he did not side with Mkhize, he was going to lose.

As a group, Mashatile's backers were united behind his ambitions, but they were numerically weak and incapable of forming a slate to get him elected. Now they were goading him to contest on the Mkhize slate. The raw thrust of their point upset him. He was deeply incensed. Kicking and screaming, he shouted at the top of his voice, "I don't want to be part of the Mkhize group." But no amount of guilt by association, no scrap of ammunition, escaped his backers. They told him that the Ramaphosa group did not want him. It was that simple: "Choose or lose," they said to him.

Meanwhile, as the Ramaphosa slate was caught in stalemate at its caucus meetings with Lamola and Mabuyane, the Mkhize camp was drumming up support outside the main conference hall, ahead of the voting.[77] "This morning, we are just here to salute you. We are here because of you," Mkhize said to loud cheers.[78] Mashatile, he announced, would be their candidate for deputy president. There might have been a little brinkmanship to this, but events would prove that it was not all show. Still, at that moment Mashatile needed persuading.

His protestations were loud enough for his backers to call a headcount gathering outside the conference hall. In a show of force, all delegates voting for the Mkhize RET faction gathered for the count. The rationale for a headcount gathering is to gauge voter sentiment and the level of unity – or disunity – within a slate ahead of an actual election. All candidates for the Top 7 positions were present. Conspicuously absent was Mashatile. One of his lobbyists acknowledged to me later that he had refused to attend the gathering because he felt that, with the Ramaphosa slate divided by in-fighting between Lamola and Mabuyane, there was a healthy number of people from the Ramaphosa camp that would vote for him because they didn't necessarily see him as a problem; they saw him as a better candidate.

Even so, my own view was that with the Ramaphosa camp firmly behind Mabuyane, Mashatile had no choice but to contest the position on a Mkhize slate. On hearing what his lobbyist had to say, I realised that Mashatile had already made up his mind to run on an Mkhize ticket. And soon enough, Mashatile began to see that the only choice he had was to side with Mkhize. It was make or break, and it was a game-changer. At the very last minute, Mashatile reluctantly found himself being swayed by his lobbyists and backers to contest the deputy presidency on the ballot of the Mkhize camp.

The gambit worked. Besides raking in the full voting block of the Mkhize group, Mashastile clearly won votes in the Ramaphosa camp, too. By the time the election results were tallied, Mashatile emerged with just over 50 per cent of the votes, receiving 2,178 against Mabuyane's 1,858 and Lamola's 315. Had there been agreement between Mabuyane and Lamola, the Ramaphosa slate might have had a different outcome. But history did not pan out that way. Paul Mashatile snookered the Ramaphosa camp and slinked into the deputy presidency.

Mashatile's weakness was, in the evolving tradition of the ANC, his strength: running for deputy president in the ANC required a certain all-out competitive character, such as Mashatile possessed; he was a politician down to his very core and surely thought about power all the time. At the top of his mind, and those of his supporters, must have been succession: choosing the next deputy president meant selecting the country's next president to succeed Ramaphosa.

But besides power, Mashatile seemed to emerge from the election a victor without clear ideas about the precise policies and actions that would be needed to move the country out of its economic quandary. In fairness, it would be an oversimplification to say that Mashatile won some of the votes in the Ramaphosa camp because of an opposing vision of South Africa's future that some allied to Ramaphosa shared. It is more likely, I think, that they needed him as a bridge between the two factions in the build-up to 2024.

By the close of Sunday, the total voting delegation was 4,446. The total votes cast during the election were 4,384. There were two ballots that were confiscated because some comrades were caught trying to take photos in voting booths and their voting status was consequently revoked.

Gwede Mantashe managed to scrape through to win the national chair with 2,062 votes to Stanley Mathabatha's 2,018 and David Masondo's 280 votes. The very coveted position, the most powerful position in the organisation by far, that of secretary general, went to Fikile Mbalula who won 1,692 votes to Pule Mabe's 1,590. Unfortunately, our hopes that Febe Potgieter would stand for one of the two deputy secretary general positions backfired. She was a former NEC member, a former Youth League secretary general and current general manager of the ANC. To our absolute shock she declined during the nomination process. This is why Gwen Ramokgopa and Tina Joemat-Pettersson emerged in the scurry to replace Potgieter. The first deputy secretary general position went to Nomvula Mokonyane, who won 2,195 votes to Joemat's 2,145. The second deputy secretary general position went to Maropene Ramokgopa with 2,273 votes. Gwen Ramokgopa (not to be confused with Maropene) won 1,809 votes to become treasurer general.

As expected, Ramaphosa won the presidency by a landslide, compared with the 2017 conference when he beat Nkosazana Dlamini-Zuma by a slim 79 votes. Zweli Mkhize won 1,897 votes to Ramaphosa's 2,476.

Edgy and defiant, the RET had come out with all guns blazing only to be defeated. Some saw the results as wildly unpredictable, but the numbers don't lie. Yet the question must be asked: was this the final extinction of the RET, factionalism and corruption in the party? On the surface, Ramaphosa had managed to navigate the very stormy waters of the ANC and had been given a stronger mandate than in 2017 to steer the ANC towards the 2024 elections and beyond. Beneath the surface, though, lurked a hidden agenda. In his bid to unite and rebuild the ANC, Ramaphosa may have put paid to factionalism, but factionalism, as we will see, was not done with him.

Seven
Mashatile's back-door presidential gambit

It was a perfect summery afternoon in December 2022, and I had been kicking around my home in Johannesburg with a comrade and confidant who regularly wandered in to shoot the breeze over drinks on quiet afternoons. But this afternoon was no ordinary day. It was a trying time for our candidate at the 55th leadership conference: with the ANC leadership contest ahead of the conference later that month hotting up and the economy reeling from the economic impact of loadshedding and soaring prices, the public target of media vitriol was none other than Cyril Ramaphosa. It was open season for criticism of his presidency and party, which was less popular than ever and faced the very real prospect, for the first time since 1994, of losing its majority at the polls in 2024.

But if rolling blackouts were already gnawing at Ramaphosa's popularity, another scandal now threatened to discredit him and maybe finish him off. Around the time I met my guest for drinks, Ramaphosa had told party leaders that he wanted to resign over a scandal that broke in early June 2022 when former State Security Agency (SSA) director general and Department of Correctional Services national commissioner Arthur Fraser walked into the Rosebank police station in Johannesburg and opened a criminal case against Ramaphosa. Like most South Africans, I came across the news in a statement, issued in Fraser's name, that had been widely circulated on social media shortly after Fraser's visit to the police station. As discussed in a previous chapter, Fraser alleged that Ramaphosa had concealed a cash robbery on 9 February 2020 at his Phala Phala farm.[79] Fraser also alleged that he had provided the police with evidence showing that Ramaphosa "failed to report the cash robbery and instead had the robbers kidnapped and bribed into silence", an allegation vehemently denied by the president.[80]

It is not my intention here to dwell in any detail on the timing of Fraser's complaint or his motives, save to say that he had been facing his own challenges since his departure from Correctional Services for unlawfully authorising the early release from prison of Jacob Zuma after serving just two months of a fifteen-month sentence for defying a court order to testify at the Zondo Commission of Enquiry. What matters for this story is that the revelation immediately set off a storm just as the ANC was preparing to head to its 55th national conference in December 2022.

ON 30 NOVEMBER, just weeks before the ANC conference and as South Africans were preparing to head into the festive season, a misconduct report by a Section 89 constitutional panel submitted to National Assembly speaker Nosiviwe Mapisa-Nqakula on the Phala Phala allegations suggested that there was a prima facie case of impeachment against the president who, the report found, might have violated the Constitution.[81] The panel was appointed by parliament to consider four charges against the president, contained in a motion by the opposition African Transformation Movement (ATM).

The mere hint of impeachment immediately set off a storm. Investors hate uncertainty, and with the prospect of Ramaphosa's removal from office and no sign of a successor who could ease their worries, they effectively put South Africa into isolation. Investors feared that a return of Zuma's power bloc could threaten reforms Ramaphosa had put in place to try to clean up the grand corruption associated with

Zuma. Markets recoiled. The rand fell off a cliff, sliding 4.2 per cent to R17.9 to the dollar on the day. It was a tangible response to the very real prospect of Ramaphosa stepping down. It was also a warning shot of what might happen were Ramaphosa to go.

The Phala Phala scandal left a dangerous vacuum at a time when the country was reeling from corruption, rolling blackouts and faltering state institutions. South Africans were desperate for leadership and stability. Their best hope at the upcoming ANC conference was Ramaphosa.

My immediate reaction was that the allegations in Fraser's statement had to be looked into and Ramaphosa's name cleared. In my mind, what was in doubt was the motives for the Section 89 probe and the timing of the release of the report. South Africa, I felt, had become a country where power struggles were settled through conspiracy and character assassination rather than policy and leadership. What is not disputed is that both Fraser and Mapisa-Nqakula, who served in Zuma's cabinet, had been slighted, removed from senior positions in government and redeployed by Ramaphosa as soon as he came to high office. For his part, I was aware that Fraser had been requesting an audience with Ramaphosa to discuss the non-renewal of his contract at Correctional Services after he was found by the Gauteng High Court in Pretoria to have unlawfully released Zuma from prison. Ramaphosa, however, had snubbed Fraser, which must have riled the former intelligence boss.

In the case of the speaker of parliament, my thoughts immediately turned to her removal by Ramaphosa from her post as minister of defence, a position she had occupied from June 2012 under Zuma until August 2021 under Ramaphosa. Besides her implication in a number of corruption scandals, including her alleged acceptance of a R5 million bribe from a defence contractor, she had undertaken a trip to Zimbabwe at the height of the Covid-19 pandemic in September 2020 to meet her counterparts in preparation for a SADC meeting. It then emerged that several members of the ANC had accompanied her in an official defence force jet; this led to a formal reprimand by Ramaphosa, who also sanctioned her by imposing a salary sacrifice for three months. But it was her removal as minister of defence and demotion to speaker of parliament that was the biggest blow.

This cast of characters suggested to me that Fraser's statement, the rush to publish the Section 89 report, despite the panel's plea for more time to do their work, and the very public manner of the speaker's presentation of the preliminary findings in the report of an impeachable offence, in full view of the media, all formed a staged performance to force Ramaphosa's resignation. Here was a presidential favourite to lead the party into the elections in 2024 with his reputation in doubt less than two weeks before the ANC's national elective conference.

Shortly after the release of the Section 89 panel report to parliament, presidential spokesman Vincent Magwenya moved swiftly to try to allay concerns. He briefed the media in Cape Town that Ramaphosa was not panicking and had spent the day in talks with senior members of the ANC. "The decision will not be rushed but made in the interest of the country and the government's stability" is all Magwenya would say.

Casting worried glances over their shoulders, the Ramaphosa camp could hardly have been prepared to look ahead at a critical time when even the most far-sighted among them would have had difficulty seeing through the fog, to the elective conference and the 2024 elections. A political hurricane was bearing down on the country, and neither Ramaphosa nor his backers in the party were prepared for it. I certainly was not.

And so, as Ramaphosa's political woes seemed to galvanise supporters of the RET faction, the president, wounded and upset, began to think that resigning might be in his best interests and those of the party for the 2024 elections.

THUS IT WAS, ON the afternoon I met my guest on the patio of my home for drinks, that the question on everyone's lips was no longer whether the ANC would survive the 2024 elections. The more pressing concern was: would Ramaphosa resign ahead of the party conference and, if not, could he be nominated for president at the conference with the parliamentary committee's report hanging over his head?

As I reflected on the Phala Phala scandal, I casually asked my guest what he thought of the possible impact on the leadership contest. It was in the nature of our informal chats that we exchanged views and ideas quite liberally. He pondered the question for a minute and then dropped a bombshell of a story that, by this time, had been circulating narrowly in ANC leadership circles but not in the public domain. It was certainly news to me.

According to the story he told me, which was subsequently corroborated by senior members I spoke to in the ANC, very soon after the Phala Phala scandal broke, a group of senior ANC comrades gathered one evening in early December at a private party held at the Saxon Hotel in Johannesburg. Among them were some of the usual suspects in the ANC who had coalesced around Paul Mashatile ahead of the December conference. Individually, they were a disparate bunch, far too concerned with their own pressing parochial worries and interests. As a group they were united behind Mashatile's political ambitions. They had come to the event, in a celebratory mood, at the urging of Mashatile.

Mashatile had, during his anti-apartheid activism in the United Democratic Front (UDF), through the 1980s, earned a reputation as a leading member of a group known as the Alex Mafia (after the name of the Johannesburg township of Alexandra). It was a reputation, perhaps unfairly, that stuck through the years after the end of apartheid; but on the day of the Saxon gathering we can imagine that reputation befitting the clannish occasion, with Mashatile in control.

His chief rival was none other than Ramaphosa and the latter's backers in the ANC NEC. Just three months before, Mashatile had come under fire from members of the NEC in a heated special meeting to oust him from the office of secretary general, a position he was occupying in an acting capacity after the suspension of Ace Magashule. Apparently NEC members argued that it was in violation of the ANC's constitution for Mashatile to act in the powerful positions of secretary general and deputy secretary general.[82] The move to remove him was triggered by Ramaphosa, who had earlier proposed that NEC member Gwen Ramokgopa should support Mashatile as his deputy in ANC Top 6 meetings. Ramaphosa went on to tell the NEC meeting that officials had agreed that Mashatile would not deliver two reports at the ANC's national conference in December.[83]

My own sources in the party have told me that the move by Ramaphosa was an indication of his concern that Mashatile had been using the office of secretary general to amass power and mobilise support for his candidacy at the December conference. This was confirmed by another NEC member, who told News24 around that time that at the centre of the fight were accusations that Mashatile was using his powerful position for his own political gain.[84] It was a sign not only of Mashatile's ambition but of his frosty relationship with Ramaphosa ahead of the December conference.

As DRINKS FLOWED AT the Saxon and the evening progressed, Mashatile was joined by others – around fifteen of his staunchest backers. They saw, in the wake of Phala Phala, the possibility of a power vacuum. With Ramaphosa's reputation damaged and his presidential poll severely weakened by the exposé, the political landscape had become increasingly chaotic. It was a time when Ramaphosa's rivals knew quite well how to get what they wanted; they had a sense of their power as a group. They had forged connections at the ANC's 2017 conference and met regularly in other places at other times since then, but never as an organised faction. Now they were consolidating around Mashatile as their presidential candidate in the build-up to the 55th conference. They must have felt they were newly minted masters of the universe whose own careers were linked to Mashatile's success in the elections. Whatever their inclination as a group, they were individually considering their best chance of retaining their power.

In Mashatile's mind, my guest told me, the gathering was to be a protected space where they would be free to talk and coalesce around a plan to revive Mashatile's fortunes in the ANC. Mashatile did not want to create a club that would be perceived as yet another faction. My guest told me that Mashatile wanted his inner circle to think broadly about how to build his power base as a unifying candidate between the Ramaphosa and RET factions.

Sometime that evening, David Mabuza, who was still deputy president at the time, and Mashatile sat down to discuss the implications of Phala Phala for Mashatile's leadership ambitions at the upcoming conference. In the course of their conversation, the two agreed that Ramaphosa was at his weakest yet. They talked late into the evening and at some point hatched a plan.

"What do you mean?" I asked my guest.

"You know, Oscar, the thing about chess games is that many moves are a result of unintended consequences. It is a strategic game. You have to make a move that triggers a move by your opponent so that you can strike," he replied.

Either by design or coincidence, the Saxon gambit came to mirror the actual outcome of conference. According to the plan, the first prize was Ramaphosa's resignation before the conference. Without a strong alternative candidate in the Ramaphosa camp, Mashatile would make a direct play for the presidency with Mabuza standing for a second term as deputy president.

But there was a Plan B: should Ramaphosa contest the presidency at the 55th conference and win, Mabuza would step down as deputy president and Mashatile would step in. But there was a twist to the scheme, far more audacious than I could have imagined at first, to take over the presidency. Mashatile would make a play for the presidency after the conference, ahead of the 2024 elections. The trigger to force Ramaphosa's resignation would be Phala Phala. That way, Mashatile would enter the presidency, being next in line in the succession chain, through the back door.

JUST HOW CLOSE PLAN A came to fruition was born out by my meeting with Northern Cape premier Zamani Saul who, as I have mentioned, relayed the details of Ramaphosa's resignation to me over dinner in Kimberley in early January 2023. It was shortly after Ramaphosa cancelled a press conference on 1 December, subsequent to a visit to his Cape Town residence by Derek Hanekom, Gwede Mantashe and other NEC members to persuade him to stay on as president, that Zamani received a call from Ramaphosa. "He said he still wanted to resign and was calling me first before calling all provincial chairs of the ANC to inform them that he intended to resign with immediate effect from the ANC and then resign as president of the Republic on the 31st of December. It would be a staged process so that there's a proper handover to a new president," Zamani told me.

At that point, Zamani asked Ramaphosa whether he had consulted with the other provincial chairpersons. Ramaphosa said he planned on phoning each individually, but Zamani interjected and suggested that Ramaphosa should include "one or two other chairpersons in a teleconference". Ramaphosa agreed to arrange a conference call with Oscar Mabuyane from the Eastern Cape and Mandla Ndlovu, the Mpumalanga provincial chair, because of their loyalty and steadfast support for his second term.

Ramaphosa wanted to keep the attention of the teleconference on a decision he'd already taken and a succession plan he wanted to put in place. For a while it seemed to have gone just as he wished. After he briefed the provincial chairs of his decision to resign, they took turns to respond. The Mpumalanga chair was first, saying it was unfortunate that it had come to that, but he supported his decision. "It is your decision, Mr President," he said. "We are going to see how we navigate the process." Then Mabuyane followed suit, saying he understood the stress the Phala Phala incident had caused and it was important that the president keep up his strength. One by one, they concurred with Ramaphosa's decision, until Zamani spoke.

Zamani had had some time to reflect not only on the report from parliament but also on the sentiments expressed at the morning's meeting between Mantashe, Hanekom and Ramaphosa as well as what the two provincial chairs were saying. Addressing Ramaphosa, he said, "You know, Mr President, I understand the pressure and the decision you have made, but I think we need to be aware of the immediate consequences of such a decision." He went on to point out that the national conference was a week away and that no other candidate was electable. "We are literally days away from the national elective conference. There is no way that a credible alternative is going to be found to stand against Mkhize," he said. Mabuyane was emphatic that Ramaphosa's resignation would simply hand the conference to the Mkhize camp.

Then he told Ramaphosa that he needed to understand that the dynamic of the Phala Phala matter had a life of its own; it was not going to disappear after he resigned. "You had better think again because these people are very vindictive, and in the same manner as President Zuma is being dragged in and out of court they are going to make sure that that is going to be the case with you, Mr President," he said. He concluded on a positive note, telling Ramaphosa that the parliamentary report was not as sound as it seemed at first. "There are flaws and gaps in the parliamentary report and it should be taken on review," he said. To which Ramaphosa asked what would happen if, upon taking it on review, he lost. "What matters is that we get through conference," Zamani said.

I suspect that a deal was struck after Zamani spoke. The clincher was likely Zamani's warning that Ramaphosa might hand the conference to Mkhize.

As he put it to me, "After that, momentum came, and everyone said the president could not leave us in the lurch. The position was, let's go to conference and let's win. The president did not only accept the fact that he would stay, but he possibly accepted something to the effect that he would go through conference and, if we prevail, he was unlikely to want to stay beyond 2024."

If my reading of Zamani's recollections is accurate, I suspect Ramaphosa insisted that he did not want to be the face of the ANC's contestation of the 2024 elections. He wanted to make a clean break and hand over to whoever was going to be his deputy, to take the ANC into the elections.

Another interpretation is that he was prepared to wait and see what the outcome of the December conference would be. If he won the leadership race, he'd take the ANC to the 2024 elections. Soon after the elections, whose outcome could involve coalition arrangements with opposition parties should the ANC lose its majority, he would step down. My own impression is that we ought to prepare for either of these possibilities.

WHEN I REFLECTED ON my conversation with Zamani, with the knowledge of Mashatile's Saxon plan, I was struck by what eventuated. Curiously, Zamani had been a supporter of Mashatile and, as things turned out, backed his candidacy for the deputy presidency at the conference. While it was pure rumour at the time this story was relayed to me, we now know that Mabuza did resign as deputy president. But there was a twist to the plot hatched at the Saxon: should Mashatile win the deputy presidency, the plan was to fast-track his ascendancy to the West Wing at the Union Buildings. The plan chimed with Ramaphosa's concerns during his teleconference with provincial chairs about the Phala Phala saga backfiring: Mashatile did have in mind giving additional weight to the Phala Phala saga after the ANC conference in his bid to force Ramaphosa out of the ANC and the presidency. All Mashatile had to do was bide his time.

The ensuing political milieu would quickly demonstrate that, with Ramaphosa limping, there would be nothing to bar Mashatile from becoming president and thus the face of the ANC in the 2024 general elections. It is worth noting that at the time of writing this chapter, former president Thabo Mbeki pulled the trigger on Phala Phala in a fifteen-page letter to Mashatile in the latter's capacity as deputy president of the ANC, in which Mbeki accused the ANC of violating the Constitution by using its majority in parliament to block committees charged with investigating the matter.[85] He implored Mashatile to take up his concerns in the interests of the party and the country.

I do not here want to discuss the merits and demerits of Mbeki's letter, save to say that we ought to recognise that Ramaphosa is the best face for the ANC in 2024 and the best chance for the party to win enough votes to negotiate from a position of strength with coalition partners. Now is not the time to change captains midstream. With a few months to the elections, it is strategically unwise to open flanks within the party and government for agitation when the party ought to be uniting for a bigger cause. In that sense, Mashatile would do well to throw his weight behind Ramaphosa by focusing on a few critical areas that have caused considerable reputational damage to the party. Indeed, the goal ought to be to show a united front in an effort to change the mindset of the electorate.

And here I want to suggest that Ramaphosa's strategic positioning of the ANC and government in the manner of Mandela should mean greater responsibilities to Mashatile as his deputy. In other words, I am suggesting that Ramaphosa has in mind a moral responsibility to float above the hurly-burly, with Mashatile running government, chairing cabinet meetings and handling the affairs of the ANC. In that sense, I see the possibility of a resolution of the tension between the president and deputy president, with Ramaphosa taking on a more managerial role in the diplomatic arena, domestically, continentally and globally at a time when South Africa's reputation has taken an enormous knock and the economy has been put into isolation. He ought, too, to revive the foreign investment drive with which he began his presidency in 2019.

It is also important to mention that if both Ramaphosa and Mashatile are to have inner circles – and it is not unreasonable to expect trusted lieutenants to coalesce around leaders in the rough and tumble of politics – those circles should close within the unifying framework of the ANC and government. There are people around the president and deputy president who, despite their personal ambitions, share the same understanding of the objectives of Ramaphosa's ANC. And here Mashatile would potentially be a centre of gravity to draw people around the party's unifying goals. He needs to be strategic and think for himself about what he wants going forward.

As I have mentioned, the ANC's mission is a long haul whose goals and objectives are to build a prosperous, non-racial and non-sexist country.

Now I want to briefly return to the Saxon plan and its implications for 2024.

EVENTS MAY NOT HAVE unfolded exactly as planned, but it came as no surprise to me that Mashatile won the deputy presidency. I have no doubt that the Saxon plan was the reason for Ramaphosa's delay in confirming Mashatile as his deputy. It was subsequently reported in the media that it was only after Ramaphosa sat down with Mashatile in what turned out to be a very long private meeting before his cabinet reshuffle that he eventually confirmed Mashatile's position.[86] The details of the meeting were not made public, but we can surmise that Ramaphosa set out the rules of engagement between the two and the bigger picture, which includes unifying the party, already reeling from divisions, around a majority victory at the 2024 polls.

Will the party bend to 2024? We now turn to the realm of analysis and prognosis in subsequent chapters, which make up Part Two of this book.

Part Two

Results and Prospects

Eight
Has the ANC fulfilled its historical mission?

When, on Sunday, 26 June 1955, about 3,000 ANC delegates of all colours and backgrounds gathered in an open veld outside Johannesburg in what the historian Saul Dubow, in his account of the event, has described as a "carnival-like show of popular strength"[87] to draft the Freedom Charter, they had in mind not ideology, but the dreams and aspirations of millions of people. Among their aspirations were the rights to share the country's wealth; to enjoy human rights and equality before the law; and to secure equal access to education, housing and medical care. These aspirations, recalled Rusty Bernstein in his memoir, *Memory and Forgetting*, were written by thousands of people on pieces of paper, scraps of cardboard and toilet paper. They were, wrote Dubow, relatively uncontroversial. "Rather more problematic were two ambiguous provisions: the statement that 'South Africa belongs to all who live in it, black and white', and the provisions to transfer into common ownership the country's mineral wealth, banks and monopoly industries."[88]

What the Freedom Charter proclaimed was a post-apartheid state that would rely on interventions to deliver the people's democratic aspirations. It strongly advocated socio-economic rights and state intervention in securing such rights. These aspirations, writes Dubow, were consistent with the development of an interventionist state based on the social rights of citizenship, capable of ensuring that economic arrangements would create full employment and giving effect to post-war social policies for a national health service, free comprehensive education and a non-stigmatising system of social security.

The state's repressive response to the upsurge of popular resistance that followed the Defiance Campaign in the early 1950s and the adoption of the Freedom Charter led to the banning of the ANC in 1960, which lasted until 1990. This period meant that the anti-apartheid struggle for universal suffrage overshadowed discussions of post-apartheid socio-economic policies.

With the unbanning of anti-apartheid organisations in 1990, there revived in the ANC a dynamic debate on post-apartheid socio-economic policy. And so, almost forty years after the adoption of the Freedom Charter, the "Ready to Govern"[89] policy document focused much of its content on the ANC's plan "to create a strong, dynamic and balanced economy". Interspersed with democratic aspirations was the language of a "mixed economy", in which the democratic state would consider increasing or reducing the public sector. The document advocated state involvement in economic activity to strengthen the ability of the government to respond to the massive inequalities in the country. And it envisioned an activist post-apartheid state with policy measures directed at "ensuring employment creation, industrial restructuring, the elimination of poverty, responding to the basic needs of the population, achieving sustainable growth and curbing monopolies".[90]

It is not my intention in this chapter to deal with the party's economic policies before its unbanning or its prospects in 2024, which I will return to in the concluding chapter. It is, rather, to understand the ANC's performance as a governing party against its policy goals since 1994 in order to answer the question: has the ANC fulfilled its historical aspirations? If I can track its historical performance since 1994, then perhaps the party's successes and failures – its attempts, in other words, to adjust its policies and practical interventions to changing conditions since 1994 – will become clearer; so, too, will its relevance

– or irrelevance as the case may be – to the very pressing challenges of the day and its prospects in 2024 and beyond.

My overall approach is to map the evolution of the ANC's policies and their outcomes since 1994 against the party's actual performance in the next chapter and then its electoral performance in the penultimate chapter. I make no claim to being an economist, and my approach is not an economic dissection or analysis of the country's macro and fiscal policies, nor is it an analysis thereof. Instead, it is a broad account of policy choices and outcomes set against electoral outcomes since 1994.

The policy evolution since 1994

Outlines of the 1994 settlement

When, in the early 1990s, the ANC and National Party engaged in talks about the terms of a settlement, some of what the ANC argued for differed significantly from the founding principles in the Freedom Charter. This meant that the constitutional settlement, enshrined in the Interim Constitution of 1993, circumscribed the role the state could ideally play in radically transforming the economy. Ultimately, the agreement rested on a system of universal suffrage, a separation of powers, multiparty elections and a Bill of Rights.

The Interim Constitution, writes Hein Marais,[91] had to comply with a set of thirty-three binding constitutional principles which crystallised important compromises agreed to in the final stages of the negotiations. Altering these principles required a two-thirds majority in parliament. They required, for instance, that

- The diversity of language and culture be protected;
- Collective rights of self-determination in forming, joining and maintaining organs of civil society be recognised and protected;
- The rights of ownership of private property be protected;
- Exclusive and concurrent powers and functions be delegated to provincial governments;
- National government be prevented from exercising its powers in ways that encroached upon the geographical, functional or institutional integrity of the principles;
- Minority parties be enabled to participate in the legislative process;

- The independence and impartiality of the Reserve Bank be protected.[92]

What these principles effectively meant was that the terms of the settlement, despite far-right bombing campaigns around that time, would "reflect the influence of forces outside the multiparty negotiations specifically"[93] – large corporate entities, for example, which would allow business to fashion a great deal of the kind of socio-economic reforms needed to drive growth and development.

Despite these limitations, the settlement represented a political milestone which, justifiably, won the admiration of the international community. A peaceful transition to the 1994 elections occurred, with historical foes agreeing to negotiate the economic transition through a series of mutually agreeable trade-offs in the national interest.

The question is whether those trade-offs represented fundamental departures from the ANC's historical mission. Here it is important to understand that the ANC always had in mind a redistribution of wealth, the eradication of racial inequality and the construction of a non-racial, non-sexist and prosperous South Africa in which all citizens, black and white, would live in harmony. The task assumed by the ANC in 1994, however, meant that some of the radical breaks with apartheid envisaged in its policies had to be postponed. But, to bring clarity to that moment, the goal remained a post-apartheid "transition", rather than rupture, that would allow divergent interests to "pass through a gateway of concessions and compromises in order to avert disaster for their respective agendas".[94] This amounted to an attempt to forge a new basis for a social contract – "an essential basis of any bid to restructure South African society", as Marais observes.[95]

Whether the terms of that social contract were along unequal or egalitarian lines is a matter of historical record. That the ANC entered the post-1994 era without dismantling the country's "two nation" character through a radical redistribution of resources, opting instead for a gradual dismantling of its institutional architecture, is now widely accepted. But that does not mean abandonment of its mission.

What matters for this analysis is whether the outcomes of a series of gradual policy adjustments since 1994 have benefited those historically excluded from political and economic life. Broadly speaking, understanding the historical record means understanding the policy evolution since 1994, to which I now turn.

Recasting the terrain: From "Ready to Govern" to the RDP

The economic views of the ANC significantly changed from, in essence, concurring with the economic views and policy prescriptions of the left in the tripartite alliance until the early 1990s, to fully embracing mainstream economic and policy prescripts within two years after the 1994 settlement. This was not an inconsequential change. It shaped the post-apartheid government's role in the economy, its economic policy choices for and constraints on the country's growth and development outcomes over the last twenty-six and more years.

What must be borne in mind is that, notwithstanding the rose-tinted lens through which the drafters of the "Ready to Govern" document imagined post-apartheid South Africa, the document did not consider the removal of imperfections, frictions and market rigidities as a way to achieve full employment, to meet the people's basic needs or to restructure South African trade and industry. Moreover, it did not view government expenditure as something that would crowd out the private sector, and thus did not consider the dependence of South Africa's future economic growth on foreign direct investment flows. In the "Ready to Govern" document, therefore, "the ANC's intent, strategy and specific economic policy ideas continued to mainly reflect a heterodox view of the South African economy".[96]

After the ANC's national conference in June 1992, which adopted the "Ready to Govern" document, the party leadership gradually gravitated towards mainstream views and policies. Initially, the ANC supported, and led, work on the Reconstruction and Development Programme (RDP) and Macroeconomic Research Group (MERG) initiatives, both of which were guided by redistributive policies on the country's future growth and development path beyond apartheid. Concurrently, the ANC leadership was engaged in economic policy issues with advocates of mainstream views and policies, such as the National Party, representatives of organised domestic capital, and international financial agencies like the International Monetary Fund (IMF).

By the end of 1993, the ANC leadership had already decided to fully distance itself from the MERG analysis and policy recommendations, and became a signatory to an IMF mainstream medium-term economic policy package, referred to as the "Statement of Policies", that accompanied an $800 million loan agreement in 1993. Even though the ANC by this time had adopted the RDP as an integral element of its manifesto for the first democratic election in 1994, the party started to distance itself from the RDP policy framework soon after the 1994 election. In the RDP White Paper, released in September 1994, six principles were subtly infused with mainstream economic views.

However, the changes to the original RDP policy framework were significant. In the original formulation the RDP followed a "growth through redistribution" policy which rested on both export promotion and inward industrialisation aimed at significantly expanding domestic demand and social infrastructure. In the RDP White Paper, the goal of redistribution was dropped as the main objective, and the government's role in the economy was reduced to the task of managing the transformation agenda. Fiscal policy would be driven by emerging concerns not to sacrifice fiscal discipline. Thus, monetary policy was set to be independent in its policy-making with no specific measures to allow for government interference.

Such thinking quickly came up against left-wing criticism, but it was, in economist Nicoli Nattrass's view, a route chosen in the specific context of the negotiations towards a constitutional settlement in the early 1990s that "served the political purpose of uniting various constituencies within the ANC" – implying, as Marias argues, "a certain degree of expediency and awareness that the policy had a short shelf life".[97]

By 1995–6, the ANC government had already moulded the RDP into a mainstream economic policy document, the analysis and policy framework of which sat closer to the IMF's 1993 "Statement of Policies" than the original RDP document. The groundwork had been laid for a decisive policy shift.

Neoliberalising development: The adoption of GEAR

When, in 1996, Thabo Mbeki, an economist by training, began convincing former ideological foes in the ANC's labour alliance of the real state of the economy and the challenges that lay ahead, he had in mind an economy reeling from debt, and desperately in need of foreign investment and growth in order to drive the ANC's redistribution agenda. Mbeki's reasoning was twofold. First, he argued that when the ANC was unbanned in 1990, it had no economic policy. Its 1988 Constitutional Guidelines and "Ready to Govern" document, as I have argued, had committed it to a mixed economy, but this was largely based on vague references to the Freedom Charter that "the people shall govern"; "the national wealth of the country, the heritage of all South Africans shall be restored to the people"; and "the mineral wealth beneath the soil, the banks and monopoly industry shall be transferred to the ownership of the people as a whole".

The ANC's first attempt to fill the policy gap was its 1990 "Discussion Document on Economic Policy", which stressed the planned initial restructuring of industry and the financial sector, along with the redirection of domestic savings into productive activity and infrastructure development. But Mbeki saw that the distance between those aspirations and economic reality was too vast to bridge with the lofty goals of the RDP. His concern by 1995 was that a growth through redistribution approach would overheat the economy and worsen its debt position. South Africa, to be sure, entered the transition with an economy reeling from a growth rate that had plunged to –1.1 per cent in the early 1990s.[98] The following key indicators, articulated by Marais, demonstrated the gravity of the crisis:

- Declining rates of gross fixed investment (which plunged as low as –18.6 per cent in 1986, and stayed negative from 1990 to 1993), and high rates of capital flight;
- Low rates of private investment, which led to the under-utilisation of manufacturing plant capacity (dropping from 90 per cent in 1981 to 78 per cent in 1993) and declining levels of competitiveness;
- Plummeting levels of personal savings, which, as a proportion of disposable income, dropped from 11 per cent in 1975 to 3 per cent in 1987;

- Very high unemployment, and the economy's inability to create enough new jobs to absorb even a fraction of new entrants into the labour market, a trend exacerbated by under-investment in labour-intensive services;
- Chronic balance of payments difficulties.[99]

In broad terms, this meant that the ANC had inherited an economy in a structural crisis, dependent on raw materials (mainly minerals), prone to exchange rate fluctuations, and reliant on imported capital goods and services, leading to balance of payments problems. The result was low investment rates, capital flight, a shortage of skilled labour and a surplus of unskilled, unemployed black labour – and, of course, unmanageable debt to GDP ratios. A number of economic scenarios presented at conferences during the political negotiations in the early 1990s had demonstrated the scale of the crisis and the limitations of various policy choices. Mbeki was all the while aware that work on the RDP tended to downplay the crisis and the growth imperative.

Convinced that redistribution would have to occur on a gradual, differential basis over a relatively longer timescale, Mbeki engineered a push towards the second policy adjustment to the post-1994 reality. In 1996, the government adopted an export-oriented growth path, dispensing with the RDP's inward-looking industrialisation strategy geared to servicing domestic redistributive needs in the first instance. In short, the "growth through redistribution" strategy was deemed unsustainable, with the "Mont Fleur scenario" likening it to the fateful flight of Icarus, warning: "After a year or two the programme runs into budgetary, monetary and balance of payments constraints. The budget deficit well exceeds 10%. Depreciations, inflation, economic uncertainty and collapse follow. The country experiences an economic crisis of hitherto unknown proportions which results in social collapse and political chaos."[100] The primary concern of Mbeki by this time was that South Africa simply lacked the advantages of East Asian economies like Malaysia and China to pursue state-led policies. The result was the Growth, Employment and Redistribution (GEAR) strategy, which leaned heavily towards supply-side measures to boost industrial performance, enhance the country's competitiveness, and restructure industry.

Among the factors that produced these setbacks, several tend to be overlooked. The left mistakenly assumed it had achieved sufficient weight within the ANC-led tripartite alliance. It also disregarded the extent to which the parameters of the RDP in practice would be drawn on the basis of setbacks suffered outside the political negotiations. Most obvious was the abandonment, first, of the growth through redistribution formula and, later, of the substitute formula of growth and redistribution. Instead, the left sought solace in the predictable rhetoric of the ANC government, which, for obvious reasons, continued to pay lip service to the transformative elements of the RDP, which, in practice, had been superseded.[101]

By mid-1997, elements within the government had begun an attempt to graft a developmental framework (based on RDP principles) on to GEAR – "a futile bid," writes Hein Marais, "since a social development programme could not be appended to (let alone be integrated with) a macroeconomic strategy characterised by privatisation, deregulation, fiscal austerity and the predominance of the financial sector over production and commerce".[102] Not only the programme's sweep but "its very character and logic had been overwritten by the regressions that were consummated in the GEAR strategy".[103] Indeed, as Marais has written, "the actual utility of the RDP as a government programme had changed dramatically".[104]

To be clear, GEAR hinged on a promise of increasing annual growth by an average 4.2 per cent, creating 1.35 million new jobs by the year 2000, boosting exports by an average 8.4 per cent per annum through an array of supply-side measures, and improving social infrastructure. The methods chosen to achieve those targets included:

- Slashing state expenditure to drive the budget deficit down to 3 per cent of GDP by 2000;
- Keeping inflation in single digits;
- Reducing corporate taxes and providing tax holidays for certain investments;
- Gradually phasing out exchange control regulations;
- Encouraging wage restraint by organised workers;

- A more flexible labour market, possibly by regenerating certain categories of unskilled work and exempting small businesses from aspects of the new labour regime; and
- Speeding up privatisation.[105]

GEAR's growth projections – from 3.5 per cent in 1996 to 6.1 per cent in 2000 – hinged on investment driven by the private sector. That was the crux of the policy. The fiscal deficit, it was argued, "crowded out private investment, drove up interest rates and reduced investor confidence".[106] Thus, fiscal restraint was needed to attract investment. The free market was viewed as the ideal way to achieve efficiency and maximise social welfare. A small government was advocated with a minimal role for the state. Deregulation was to be promoted because labour, capital and other regulations were regarded as hindrances to the otherwise full employment tendency of the market.

The shift to state intervention: ASGISA

In his May 1998 speech on nation-building, President Thabo Mbeki famously declared South Africa was a country of two nations. "One of these nations is white, relatively prosperous, regardless of gender or geographic dispersal ... The second and larger nation ... is black and poor."[107]

Six years later, in his May 2004 State of the Nation address, Mbeki embroidered on the notion of two nations. Embedded in the two-economies thesis was the concept of a developmental state acting by way of strategic interventions to address the concerns of both the first and second economies in an interconnected way through growing attention to microeconomic reform, transfer payments to the vulnerable, and skills development initiatives.[108] To put that in perspective, GEAR advanced trickle-down economics, where the proceeds of growth were, at least notionally, expected to address socio-economic development challenges. By eliminating "dissavings", it was envisaged that more resources for public and private investment would be released.[109] By this economic logic, high investment would in turn lead to a higher national income and employment. Thus, GEAR saw prudent fiscal policy as a means towards development and the reduction of poverty and inequality.[110]

The government claimed that GEAR's "integrated approach" would create an average of 400,000 jobs annually, achieve an annual growth rate of 6 per cent by 2000, boost exports by an average 8.4 per cent per annum, and drastically improve social infrastructure. Accordingly, it was believed that redistribution would emerge from a trickling down of jobs and more focused public expenditure.[111]

Conversely, there were no specific measures and instruments to guarantee the private sector's assigned duty of productive investment. Nor for that matter was there any focus on developing skills to meet the human capabilities and employment challenges of industrial growth. To be sure, between 1995 and 2002 about 1.6 million net new jobs were created in the South African labour market – an average growth rate of about 2.1 per cent per annum. However, more than half a million jobs were lost as a result of the introduction of labour-saving technologies by business, increased outsourcing, and a determined shift towards casual and contract labour.[112]

By the early 2000s, the drift back to earlier theorisations of the developmental state thus "crystallised as a wide-ranging discussion in government on the expansion of services by a state capable of taking forward a far-reaching agenda of national economic development, whilst at the same time placing people and their involvement at the centre of this process".[113] Discussions of a pro-poor, interventionist (or developmental) programme prompted the state to introduce the Accelerated and Shared Growth Initiative of South Africa (ASGISA).

Thus the government's developmental interventions from the early 2000s were part of a broader approach to reduce poverty and increase unemployment.[114] Indeed, as Salim Akoojee and Simon McGrath argued in 2005, many of the interventions in education and training for the first economy could "only make sense in the context of a virtuous cycle of educational and economic development progressing together".[115] In this approach, poverty reduction in the second economy was to be addressed through an expansion of transfer payments and through an extension of services by the state, often in partnership with NGOs.

The drift to a developmental state: The NDP

By the time new political leadership under President Jacob Zuma took office in 2009, the ANC's election manifesto tended towards more decisive economic interventions in the national interest: "One of the defining features of a developmental state is the state's intervention in the economy in favour of the needs of society as a whole. A key instrument for state intervention will be a state-led industrial policy programme that will guide key aspects of economic transformation, supported by an appropriate and sustainable macro-economic policy stance, as well as trade and labour market policies."[116] Specifically, the manifesto flagged as an urgent issue and a blueprint for economic development the state's capacity to intervene through the implementation of massive industrial programmes, and stressed "the centrality of coordinating state-guided strategies towards engaging key stakeholders in an inclusive process towards the implementation of key aspects of economic transformation grounded in a sustainable macro-economic and labour market policy."[117]

In his political report to the ANC's 2010 National General Council (NGC), President Zuma indicated that "the new growth path must start with the recognition that, on the one hand, we have had economic growth for a sustained period since the advent of democracy, with particularly high growth since the early 2000s and net job creation. On the other hand, poverty remains high; inequalities have remained the same and even grown worse, while some of the jobs created often brought low wages and poor conditions".[118]

The New Growth Path (NGP) was the result. It too was concerned that some of the jobs created were low-wage forms of employment. The nucleus of the NGP, then, was a developmental state that would enhance the labour-absorption capacity of the economy and find ways to connect knowledge and innovation to the challenge of growth and new jobs. It stressed as priority areas the knowledge economy, the green economy, the manufacturing sector, the social economy and cooperatives.[119]

At least partially in response to the challenge, Zuma in 2009 appointed the National Planning Commission (NPC), comprising a team who shared the vision and principles of the democratic movement, to develop a diagnostic report. Drawing on the findings of its Diagnostic Report, released in June 2010, the NPC identified as priority interventions the following nine challenges:

1. Too few people work.
2. The standard of education for most black learners is of poor quality.
3. Infrastructure is poorly located, under-maintained and insufficient to foster higher growth.
4. Spatial patterns exclude the poor from the fruits of development.
5. The economy is overly and unsustainably resource-intensive.
6. A widespread disease burden is compounded by a failing health system.
7. Public services are uneven and often of poor quality.
8. Corruption is widespread.
9. South Africa remains a divided society.[120]

Four more pressing challenges were subsequently added: social protection, the rural economy, citizens' safety, and South Africa in relation to the southern African region and to the world.

South Africa, in the NPC's diagnosis, was in need of "a long-term perspective, focus and determination to realise our vision".[121] Rather than relying on macroeconomic levers to achieve growth targets, the NPC focused on deeper structural impediments to inclusive growth. The most significant, and perhaps radical, formulation was a reorientation of strategic priorities linked to the state's ability to play a catalytic, facilitating role in the commanding heights of the economy that would lead to development and a more equitable distribution of resources. In this regard, the ANC saw the developmental state agenda as one that would enable South Africa to play a role in the global market through increased foreign trade and foreign investment. All this would allow the state to focus on building the international competitiveness of the economy through multinational corporations formed and managed by South Africans.

Subsequent to these processes, ideas were crystallised in November 2011 in the form of the National Development Plan's Vision 2030, a long-term strategic framework within which more detailed planning could take place towards the achievement of a range of overarching strategic goals by 2030. The guiding philosophy of the NDP can be summarised as a "virtuous cycle" of expanding opportunities, growth, employment and development. Indeed, in this reasoning many of the interventions in the first economy could "only make sense in the context of a virtuous cycle of social and economic development progressing together".[122] In this approach, growth was to be accompanied by poverty alleviation interventions through an expansion of transfer payments and an extension of services by the state.

The success of the NDP has therefore depended on sustainable outcomes. The object has been to ensure particular policies and activities of priority sectors were aligned to the NDP. Unfortunately, much of the statist approach in the NDP exposed implementation weaknesses that were exploited by the state capture agenda, which entailed the looting of state resources by Zuma and a network of senior government officials.

The post-Zuma era: Ramaphosa's reforms

In 2019, National Treasury published a strategy document that also heavily used the growth diagnostic approach for its analysis and policy recommendations. However, contrary to the earlier plans, the document did not claim that the implementation of its recommendations would lead to high rates of economic growth and employment. In fact, the document's quantification section showed that the plan was likely to add only an estimated 2.3 percentage points to the baseline growth of 1.5 per cent and create one million jobs over a ten-year period, which is far short of the 10 million jobs needed.[123]

Two years later, a joint National Treasury, World Bank and IMF estimate of the impact of the National Treasury's recommendations showed that the average annual economic growth, including the baseline growth, would be 1.5 per cent between 2022 and 2026, with the unemployment rate gradually increasing to 38.3 per cent by 2026.[124] In their 2021 report for the Treasury, a team of international economists confirmed the constraints identified in the National Treasury 2019 document and basically made similar recommendations without predicting that their implementation would produce accelerated economic growth and employment.[125] On the contrary, the report included a grim outlook for the economy.

Thus, the government's long-standing conviction that the removal of binding constraints would lead to medium- to long-term accelerated economic growth and employment has, since 2019, given way to the current understanding that even with all identified constraints removed, the economy would still be stuck in low growth and high unemployment. This shift in the government's macroeconomic outlook represents a major contradiction between its earlier promise of achieving an average annual growth rate of more than 5 per cent, reducing the unemployment rate to 6 per cent and eradicating poverty by 2030, and its current expectations of low economic growth and the worsening of an already high unemployment rate over the next five years.[126]

To a large extent, the ANC government is standing at a historically important crossroad. It needs to decide whether to continue the economic views and policies of the post-2007 growth path, which the party now knows will not deliver the levels of economic growth and employment needed, or to learn from other countries that have used heterodox economic views and policies over the past fifty years to influence the working of market economies and achieved much better outcomes.

Ramaphosa, for his part, seems to have taken steps to reorientate the economic policy agenda to the pre-2007 period. His 2022 State of the Nation speech concentrated on investment and growth, the top priority being revenue to fund social grants. By 2023 there were 18 million people on social grants in South Africa. The original emphasis on BEE had essentially drawn some black professionals into wealth and propped up a small black middle class, but the distributive effects of growth had so far been unequal.

Neither fiscal nor monetary authorities have presented any evidence that the current suite of supply-side measures will improve economic and developmental outcomes. In fact, as stated earlier, the government seems to pursue the current economic policy path, knowing that on the current trajectory growth is projected to linger at 1.5 per cent and less during the 2022–6 period and the unemployment rate is expected to rise to 38.3 per cent by 2026. Furthermore, National Treasury's projections show that policies that have been advanced to increase savings and investment, reduce government dissavings and improve the debt to GDP ratio are once again expected to disappoint.

A balance sheet of progress and challenges

Since GEAR, the government's fiscal policy strategy has pursued at least two aims: to avoid permanent increases in the overall tax burden and to use medium-term deficit targets to eliminate government dissaving. In practice, these aims have constrained the government's ability to raise taxes or borrow as part of financing the expected post-apartheid socio-economic transformation.

Fiscal policy data from the last twenty-five years show the implementation of this framework has been successful. According to the economist Asghar Adelzadeh. "between 1996 and 2019 the government's total annual revenue was on average equal to 24 percent of GDP, and the annual deficit to GDP ratio was on average 3 percent. That meant the size of the government's annual expenditure was on average equivalent to 27 percent of GDP." The overwhelming emphasis has been on bringing down the fiscal deficit to address low economic growth and rising unemployment, poverty and inequality.[127]

At the same time, the mainstream fiscal strategy has, in essence, been different from that proposed in the "Ready to Govern" policy document, which stated that in a democratic South Africa "the budget fits into an overall development plan".[128] Consequently, relative to OECD countries, the South African government has spent less on delivering public goods and services and providing social protection over the past few decades. This is contrary to the myth the South Africa had become a nanny state. It has also had a negative impact on government's ability to counterbalance the country's uneven development, poverty, and income and wealth inequality. This implies that if the government's main concern has been to eliminate government debt, it came at the cost of its ability to raise revenue. And that has significantly benefited the country's well-off classes. In reality, this policy has been at the expense of the majority of South Africans, who have had to endure its direct negative impact.

The common argument for this policy stance has been that the greater the economy's savings, the greater its investment level. Therefore, measures that help raise savings will automatically help private investment. But the tool used to curb expenditure has been high real interest rates. Unfortunately, this monetary tool has inversely impacted on private investment and, according to some analysts, has limited investment and therefore growth.

According to official data from Statistics SA, the South African economy grew at an average annual rate of 2.8 per cent between 1996, when GEAR was introduced, and 2019, the year before the Covid-19 pandemic. During these years, the economy went through at least four periods: the GEAR extended period of 1996–2003, the ASGISA period of 2004–7, the international financial crisis period of 2008–9, and the NDP period of 2010–19.

In terms of actual outcomes, the government succeeded in institutionalising restrictive fiscal and monetary policies, but the policies did not produce the promised outcomes in terms of economic growth, employment and exports. South Africa's economic growth outcome did not improve much until the ASGISA period, when the average annual real GDP growth almost doubled, from 2.8 per cent during the GEAR period (1996–2000) to 5.2 per cent between 2004 and 2007. What helped this improved outcome were significant increases in public and private expenditures. This included substantial growth in public investment, especially investment by public corporations.[129]

GEAR, to be sure, served its purpose as a stabilisation measure. It was not necessarily a redistribution strategy, but rather an emergency programme to bring the country's debt down to acceptable levels. The global economic recession of the late 2000s was a game-changer in South Africa, and led to the collapse of South Africa's non-gold real exports from a high average annual growth rate of 8.8 per cent during ASGISA to 7.3 per cent during 2008–9.[130]

What is important to note is that during this period, real public investment continued to grow, especially investment by public enterprises, leading once again to a strategy of fiscal restraint. As a result, during the ten-year period after the international financial crisis, the average rate of economic growth dropped to 1.7 per cent as expenditure overtook investment.

Unemployment consequently rose from 16.4 per cent in 1995 to 28.7 per cent by 2019. According to the Quarterly Labour Force Survey (QLFS), the official unemployment rate reached 35.3 per cent during the fourth quarter of 2021.[131] The largest casualty was manufacturing, which saw a drop in the total share of employment from 15.6 per cent in 1996 to 10.8 per cent in 2019.[132]

Since 2019, the South African government has embarked on a more austere version of its post-1996 macroeconomic policies. This means that the growth of the government's planned total expenditure should be below the expected rate, to cushion the blow in poverty and inequality.

So, has the ANC fulfilled its historical mission?

Cyril Ramaphosa won the ANC presidency in 2017 on a "reform, rebuild and reunite" ticket. In government, he has reformed and rebuilt – not fast enough, not nearly decisively enough, but steadily. There has been some solid progress, especially in terms of restoring the institutional independence of key agencies of the state, such as the National Prosecuting Authority and the South African Revenue Service.

Progress on economic recovery has been weak, partly as a result of externalities such as the Covid-19 pandemic and geopolitical insecurity, but also partly because of Ramaphosa's lack of strategic vision and a weak cabinet. But how much of his term can be judged by the yardstick of the ANC's rapid decline since Zuma took office in 2009? Understanding the ANC's decline has to be measured against its history, principles, traditions and vision. But it also has to be measured against the sort of adjustments that have had to be made along the party's journey towards its vision.

The present moment is one of profound crisis in the party and economy. At the ANC's 55th national conference in Nasrec in December 2022, talk of policy and ideology was conspicuously absent. The ANC is, instead, consumed by power and patronage, and the contest between those who are corrupt and those who want to do something about corruption. There has been little space for anything else.

If Ramaphosa is willing to seize the moment and sustain the momentum since he bounced back from the brink of political disaster, then he could escape the drag factor of his own party. And here we must keep in mind that his rise in 2018, in the context of the party's decline and economic ruin, was in one sense a last-ditch effort to save the party from terminal decline. In that sense his presidency has always been inseparable from the declining fortunes of the party. His successes and failings will be measured by his ability to resolve the massive economic crisis in the country and the scourge of factionalism and corruption in his party.

The final question that must be asked is whether the ANC has negotiated the transition since 1994 with the interests of historically deprived black people in mind. That is not easy to answer given the contradictions it has had to navigate. And here we need to see the party's long walk through various phases. The very establishment of the ANC was important in giving voice to the black majority in South Africa after the white-dominated Union was formed in 1910. Beyond 1994, the task was to resolve some of the pressing economic challenges inherited from the apartheid government, principally the country's massive debt.

Whether the party has managed to balance the need for investment and growth against its redistribution priorities is an evolving narrative. I want to suggest that the party's historical mission is thus a journey rather than a destination. Along the way there have been successes and failures. But, overall, the party has succeeded in creating greater inclusion. The mere fact that we can speak of a black middle class is testimony to this. I have argued earlier in this book that the ANC's mission was always to occupy the middle ground against the radical inclinations of the left and the right-wing tendencies of those who would prefer to return the country to its racially exclusive past.

For reasons already stated, much of the policy evolution since 1994 has set the boundaries of permissible change. These changes and constraints have had unintended consequences, however. They have recast the terrain of social alliances as a basis for unity in the ANC. Meeting these challenges of dealing with the policy and political dilemmas that confront the ANC has had electoral consequences for the party and its ability to mobilise its support base, to which I now turn.

Nine
From growth to decline

When, sometime in the 1990s, Nelson Mandela cautioned his own party leadership that if the black majority did not benefit from the post-1994 transition, they would do to the ANC what they did to apartheid, he could have been talking about the present moment. The words were uttered by Mandela, but they were in fact written by Thabo Mbeki. Years later Mbeki would embroider the same caveat as an overarching theme in his own presidential speeches, warning of an explosion of social contestation if the basic demands of the poor were not met speedily enough.

The ANC has not necessarily collapsed under the impact of its own restive constituency, but the comments by Mandela and Mbeki highlight an important but under-theorised explanation for the ANC's declining fortunes: rather than exploding, the party has wilted over the years, gradually fracturing through factional splits and splinters. My purpose in this chapter is to track the ANC's decline over the years against defining moments that I think more accurately situate its electoral performance in the transition.

Since the end of the Mandela administration, a deluge of books, academic literature and media reportage has sought to narrate the electoral performance of the ANC in relation to other parties and the shifting electoral landscape. This sort of reasoning is not technically incorrect. Electoral arithmetic teaches us that one party's rise is, in theory, another's decline. However, I suggest that popular interpretations of electoral trends have long lacked precision. Instead, I want to argue that voting outcomes at the polls correspond to policy choices and institutional changes that have marked out various periods in South Africa, mirroring assertions by economists like Alan Hirsch that electoral outcomes in South Africa have tracked periods of growth and economic decline.

Building on this type of reasoning, I suggest in this chapter a more precise conceptualisation of electoral trends. I see electoral decline as a result of periods of policy adjustment by the government when there was sharp contestation within the ANC between contending interests. This has typically occurred when constituency interests have called into question the policy environment and "rules of the game" – the institutional arrangements. In particular, three elements need to receive attention: the role of policy adjustments and growth, the role of policy adjustments and social contestation, and finally the fact that voter fluidity is a cumulative process.

Understanding the ANC's decline

To map these changes over time, I explore policy shifts in South Africa from 1994 to 2019. The year 1994 marks the first democratic election in South Africa and the beginning of a period of profound institutional transformation. By 2019, the failure of many post-apartheid reforms was becoming apparent, triggering a new set of challenges. I therefore do not extend my analysis beyond 2019.

The ANC's electoral fortunes since 1994 have followed three phases of policy adjustment that coincide with two broad periods of abrupt leadership change. These phases resulted in fundamental changes in institutions, policy volatility and societal contestation. Thus, if episodes of contestation become more frequent or intense, we see adjustments or reforms, where a reprioritisation of interests results in massive political realignments. This sort of approach allows us to conceptualise the ANC's electoral performance as an evolving narrative, from growth to institutional weaknesses and failure. Taken together, the phases have resulted in the ANC's electoral decline that now prefigures a crossroads for the party: either it introduces reforms that resolve the crisis or it faces a sharp decline.

Overview of the changing landscape

To recap, in order to map changes since 1994 I explore the ANC's performance between 1994, which marks the first democratic elections in South Africa and the beginning of a period of profound institutional and policy changes and growth, and 2018 when the presidency of Cyril Ramaphosa took office after nine years of state madness under Jacob Zuma.

After an initial period of growth and institutional and policy change under Mandela and Mbeki, South Africa entered a period of nine lean years under Zuma characterised by state capture and the onset of massive misalignments in the institutions that form the state. Zuma's presidency also featured a more rapid decline in the capacity and performance of state enterprises and acute service delivery problems. Zuma's removal in 2018 inaugurated a period of reforms by Ramaphosa. It also coincided with a profound crisis during the Covid-19 pandemic and the breakdown of strategic institutions of the state such as Eskom. The net effect was a sharp decline in investment, massive employment losses, rising prices and popular anger. The accompanying table highlights the political and economic state of the country over time.

Milestones	Socio-economic context	Economic results
The pre-1994 transition: 1989–1994	• De Klerk unbans the ANC and frees Mandela after 27 years in prison. • Twenty-seven political organisations and government representatives sign the National Peace Accord, paving the way for negotiations about ending apartheid. • De Klerk dismantles SA's nuclear weapons. • The global community starts re-engaging with SA. • Various ANC members return from exile to assume leadership positions. • The assassination of Chris Hani, leader of the SA Communist Party, nearly leads to the breakdown of the process of negotiation.	• Economic collapse is imminent as a result of economic slowdown and rapidly increasing debt levels. • Average economic growth=0.57% p.a. • Average inflation rate=12.83% p.a. • Budget deficit=–6.78% of GDP.

Milestones	Socio-economic context	Economic results
The post-1994 reform context: 1994–1999	• The ANC wins the first democratic elections with close to a two-thirds majority. • SA rejoins international bodies like the Commonwealth, World Health Organization and United Nations as well as various international sporting bodies. • The Truth and Reconciliation Commission, chaired by Nobel laureate Archbishop Desmond Tutu, is established to deal with crimes under apartheid. • SA's progressive constitution is signed into law. • The Constitutional Court outlaws the death penalty. • Reintegration of South Africa into the global economy and liberalisation of the economy.	• Economic focus on meeting basic needs of those previously deprived under apartheid and equitable distribution of public spending. • Average economic growth=2.68% p.a. • Average inflation rate=7.62% p.a. • Budget deficit=–4.31% of GDP

Milestones	Socio-economic context	Economic results
The Polokwane moment: 1999–2008	• Mbeki assumes a leading role as diplomat in Africa. • The first major post-apartheid corruption scandal is exposed, an arms deal • The GEAR (Growth, Employment And Redistribution) policy with a focus on stabilisation, reduction of debt and market reforms is championed by Mbeki. • Mbeki attracts widespread criticism for his AIDS denialism and slow action in authorising treatment as HIV infection rates among pregnant women increase from 22% to 30%. • SA engages in "quiet diplomacy" with Mugabe, while millions of Zimbabweans flee to SA as the Zimbabwean economy collapses. • Xenophobic attacks leave 42 foreigners dead and thousands displaced. • Zuma, the deputy president, is implicated in corruption changes and (unsuccessfully) tried for rape. • The emphasis increasingly moves to increasing public investment and infrastructure spending in later years.	• Average economic growth=4.00% p.a. • Average inflation rate=5.92% p.a. • Budget deficit=–0.57% of GDP

Milestones	Socio-economic context	Economic results
State capture: 2009–2018	• Long-time ANC leader Patrick Lekota founds the Congress of the People in opposition to the election of Zuma as president. • The government introduces large-scale provision for antiretrovirals for HIV-infected South Africans. • The Nkandla scandal highlights Zuma's use of state funds for the development of his private residence. • Zuma lambasts "clever blacks" for valuing Western society over traditional customs. • Malema, the leader of the ANC Youth League, is expelled from the ANC for not honouring instructions from the party. He founds a new political party, the Economic Freedom Fighter in 2013. • The Marikana massacre takes place.	• Various economic plans are introduced with conflicting agendas indicative of the contested economic policy and the rise of populist agendas. • Growing corruption and problems of governance within state-owned enterprises. • Large-scale electricity blackouts take place. • Average economic growth=2.04% p.a. • Average inflation rate=6.70% p.a. • Budget deficit=–3.86% of GDP

Electoral milestones and policy adjustments since 1994

Growth, 1994–2007

When South Africa entered the transition, the effects of inherited weaknesses were in plain view. The 1994 election was a landslide triumph for the ANC because of its status as a liberation movement and because of the unifying basis of the Reconstruction and Development Programme (RDP). As the economist Brian Levy and others have written:

The 1994 democratic settlement in South Africa offered a compelling example of the existence – beneath a political discourse preoccupied with interests and policies – of an unstated assumption about a central underlying idea: that a thriving future could be built around cooperation and thus create the possibility of win-win outcomes with shared benefits. The ANC's 1994 electoral slogan – "a better life for all" – and its detailed economic electoral manifesto, the Reconstruction and Development Programme (RDP), were evidence of this thinking.[133]

The RDP, wrote Levy, "took as its point of departure a vision that reconstruction and development would be achieved through the leading and enabling role of the state, a thriving private sector, and active involvement by all sectors of civil society which in combination will lead to sustainable growth".[134]

The speed with which the old order fell and was replaced by a new one was remarkable. It appeared for a moment that a zero-sum game had become a win-win solution. As Levy puts it: "Out of a disastrous history, almost miraculously, a 'rainbow nation' of equal citizenship for South Africans of all ethnicities and colours – not merely the white minority that had long held the reins of power – was born. Its date of birth was April 27, 1994, the day South Africa's voters went to the polls in the country's first democratic election."[135] Levy explains the acceptance of the settlement by the ANC's left-wing allies involved a "tolerance of disparities",[136] built on an expectation that they would be resolved. Acceptance of imbalances, however, was not unconditional; it certainly was not indefinite. Although the iconic status of Nelson Mandela offered hope of building a foundation for peace and stability on an ethos of racial reconciliation, the economic problems facing the country meant confronting hard realities in a way that was unacceptable to the ANC's left-wing allies in the alliance.

The country's large debt to GDP ratio, low investment rates, chronic balance of payments difficulties, and unacceptable levels of unemployment and inequality created policy dilemmas within the tripartite alliance. The prospect of institutions and ideas built on cooperation may have been seductive to opposing parties wishing for peace and stability, but the design of policies and institutions would sooner or later have to decide how to accommodate the ideals of the RDP, which, as I have argued, was centred on a redistribution of resources.

For the country's white minority, these institutions had long provided a robust economic, social and political governance framework; the transition to democracy extended these to the population as a whole. The guaranteeing of those institutions, including the protection of private property rights and group rights, was a policy requirement if the economy was to be an attractive environment for much-needed investment. In 1996 the new Constitution entrenched property rights. Thus, while the new political order was based on the principle of equal citizenship for all, the constitutional protection of the rights of all citizens as individuals – consistent with the non-racial ethos of the ANC – created policy dilemmas. As Alan Hirsch (then South Africa's chief director of economic policy within the Office of the Presidency) summarised in his book *Season of Hope*, the "crucial challenge was to combine a commitment to growth with a commitment to sharing the benefits of that growth ... The effort to combine growth and redistribution required a collective, society-wide commitment – one that cut profoundly against the grain of South Africa's historical legacy."[137]

In response, the ANC abandoned the RDP and introduced the neoliberal Growth, Employment and Redistribution (GEAR) plan as a series of market- and growth-led adjustments, including the liberalisation of trade and labour markets, privatisation and deregulation, and exchange control relaxation. Gradually, gains began to be evident; debt declined and the economy grew modestly. According to Levy,

> In the first dozen years of democracy, as confidence in the new system took hold, growth began to accelerate. Indeed, signalling the private sector's rising confidence, private investment gradually rose as a share of GDP from an average of about 14 percent in the 1990s to 17 percent in 2007. Growth provided the fiscal means for addressing absolute poverty; the growing

economy also offered new opportunities for expanding the middle class and for upward mobility via the private sector. In the absence of growth, however, everything else would become more difficult – as South Africa would discover in time.[138]

In the early years of democracy, the extension of services was a major focus. Between 1994 and 2003, as a central goal of the RDP, more than 1.5 million houses were built for the poor. Access to potable water grew from 60 to 80 per cent of households between 1998 and 2003, and access to electricity grew from 50 to 70 per cent of households between 1994 and 2000.[139]

Beginning in the latter 1990s, as government finances strengthened, South Africa greatly expanded its social grants. Pension payments (which during apartheid years had been generous for white South Africans) were universalised and equalised. A Child Support Grant, the main form of support for indigent families, was introduced in 1998 and had reached three million children by 2003.[140]

The growth phase lasted roughly nine years. But the conditions for growth were created through extreme measures that did not favour those on the margins of the economy. Indeed, achieving gains in growth turned out to be the relatively easy part of the agenda of building a thriving inclusive society. "Addressing other dimensions of exclusion and inequality turned out to be more difficult – and the lack of resolution in these other dimensions placed new pressure on institutions," wrote Hirsch.[141] For all of the above gains, there were some stark limitations on the progress experienced by those at the bottom of South Africa's distributional pyramid.

The poorest four deciles were largely unemployed or underemployed and were found mostly in rural areas (designated as "reserves" or "homelands" in the apartheid era) and informal settlements around towns and cities. Gains for the poorest 40 per cent were achieved without much alteration to their difficult underlying realities. Against this, the successful containment of expectations and instability, driven by hope, formed the basis of a consensus within the ANC alliance that sustained large victories at the polls both in 1994 and at the end of the Mandela presidency by the close of the 1990s.

Recognising that newly empowered political elites were unlikely to be satisfied with a shift in formal political authority if there was next to no change in economic power, by the early 2000s the ANC's focus shifted more stridently towards policies centred on Black Economic Empowerment (BEE), which some have argued was necessary for the creation of a black elite but had unintended consequences for the poor.

Since the introduction of the BEE Codes in the early 2000s, following the recommendations of the BEE Commission established by Thabo Mbeki, the economic benefits have tended to go to a tiny fraction of the black population. The challenge had two distinct aspects: the reliance on elite bargains between black and white capital, and the reliance on the state in later years as the primary mode of drawing blacks into business. The result was the exclusion of the black majority from access to resources and opportunities.

Within the private sector it seemed, at first glance, as if South Africa was experiencing ideal conditions. Yet the rapid changes in institutions in the 1990s triggered a flood of outbound foreign investment as firms sought to dramatically reduce their exposure to the country. The relaxation of exchange controls saw large white-owned companies such as the media firm Naspers moving their assets abroad. In the 1990s, investment went primarily to advanced economies in Europe and increasingly also North America. Long before the dual exchange system was abolished, numerous South African firms had acquired an international holding company or subsidiary that they could use to facilitate internationalisation. And even when a firm did not yet have an international base, by now a large network of personal and historical ties existed that could support internationalisation. Most notably, in 1999 Anglo American merged with its international holding arm, Minorco, and shifted its primary listing to the London Stock Exchange. All these factors suggest that the 1996 policy shift and the growth spurt came at huge costs.

Decline, 2007–2017

The inauguration of Jacob Zuma as president in May 2009 marked the second phase of policy adjustment. These adjustments were a response to rising disgruntlement among the ANC's rank and file constituency with the outcome of the democratic settlement and the 1996 policy change with GEAR. The early 1990s to 2007 was marked by a period of intensifying societal instability as well as reforms to institutional arrangements which created tensions in the tripartite alliance. While it is clear why intensifying societal instability would result in policy reforms, the evidence from South Africa suggests that institutional reforms had a similar effect. This is because even limited reforms introduced uncertainty by suggesting changeability in the institutional environment. Given the push for changes in the shape or form of the economy, an alliance of labour and the ANC Youth League was mobilised against Mbeki, with Jacob Zuma as its face. The result was nothing short of a coup at the ANC's national conference in Polokwane in 2007 and the subsequent election of an interim government under Motlanthe.

The ANC's electoral conferences can be pivotal moments in shaping the country's future. The 2007 Polokwane conference was one. When Zuma took office, many who backed him hoped that he would bring an inclusive, coalition-building, popular touch to leadership, in contrast to Mbeki's remote, technocratic and somewhat imperious style. In the event, Zuma proved to be a cunning, ruthless and charismatic tactician.

The 2007 conference marked the defeat of the ANC's post-1994 governing establishment and its guiding vision. The divisions this created within the ANC resulted in splits and the formation of a new breakaway party, COPE. The national election the following year was therefore marked by the onset of decline in the electoral fortunes of the ANC, driven by profound political and policy instability and institutional decay, though at this stage the shifting electoral landscape was contained.

New policy reforms under Zuma that had a veneer of radicalism – including the push for the nationalisation of strategic centres of power such as the Reserve Bank and the expropriation of land – created more instability between 2009, when Zuma became president, and the next national election in 2014. After 2010, there was a new dynamic: the capture of state resources by a network of individuals connected to Zuma. While the policy appeal to "radical economic transformation" gained an echo among the poor, in practice it was a pretext for state capture.

The result was a handful of individuals benefiting from the looting of state assets. The period 2010–17 was also characterised by levels of flight capital not experienced since the early 1990s, as most wealthy South Africans saw reforms during this period as attempts to expropriate private property. Business by now openly criticised Zuma. Within the ANC, rank and file members quickly began to see that radical economic transformation was an elite agenda to loot from the state. While some benefited from social grants, most were left out of the loop.

During this phase the ANC experienced its most dramatic fall in support since 1994, shown in its loss of various metros in the country to opposition parties during the 2016 local government election. Meanwhile, media reportage of state capture and Zuma's personal implication in unlawful upgrades of his Nkandla homestead seem to have brought the entire ANC leadership into disrepute. In essence, as Brian Levy has noted, during the Zuma presidency "the focus of efforts at elite transformation shifted away from BEE initiatives to reshape ownership and control of the business establishment and toward the repurposing of SOEs. This change created new pressures for South Africa's institutions of accountability."[142]

The 2016 *State of Capture* report issued by Thuli Madonsela, the head of South Africa's Office of the Public Protector, provided details of state capture that had adverse consequences for the reputation of the ANC. How and why the governance of South Africa's SOEs took a different turn is spelled out in compelling detail in the 2016 *Betrayal of the Promise* report. Here is how the authors put it:

> Jacob Zuma's presidency has been aimed at repurposing state institutions to consolidate a Zuma-centred power elite ... These [Zuma-centred] networks are pursuing two aims. The first is to drive a transition from traditional BEE, which was premised on the possibility of reforming the white-dominated economy, to "radical economic transformation" driven by

groups disguised as a black capitalist class independent of white monopoly capital. The second is to drive a transition from acceptance of the constitutional settlement and the "rules of the game" to a repurposing of state institutions that is achieved, in part, by breaking those rules .... The battleground for economic transformation was shifting away from the economy itself to the state and, specifically, to SOEs that outsourced massive industrial contracts to private-sector service providers ... [This required] preferential procurement from black-owned companies.[143]

Over his nine years in office, Zuma governed in an increasingly personalised way, with increasing recourse to polarising rhetoric. Unsurprisingly, given the country's fraught history, there was a distinctly racial flavour to South Africa's angry turn. Moreover, the inner workings of the ANC alliance resulted in a pattern of decision-making that disproportionately empowered unionised blue- and white-collar workers at the expense of those of its supporters who were outside the formal economy.

Whatever the origins of the problem, its continued persistence made it difficult for the ANC government to deliver on its promise of upward mobility. It faced an especially difficult tension between creating new opportunities for those outside the formal economy and satisfying the concerns of vulnerable black middle-class insiders, who were an influential bloc within the ANC. One notable institutional consequence of the pressure to expand the black South African middle class was noted by Levy: "In the absence of a thriving, market-driven ladder of opportunity, public sector employment became an important pathway to upward mobility. Insofar as this shift has been combined with a rising propensity to patronage and clientelism, the public sector has had to contend with growing pressures on the fiscus and on service quality."[144]

The cumulative consequence has been a cascading set of knock-on pressures, a slowdown in growth, and an accelerating downward spiral of support for the ANC.

Between failure and reform, 2018–2022

The third phase of decline coincided with the end of the Zuma presidency and the reforms of the Ramaphosa administration between 2018, when Zuma resigned, and 2022. We recall that Ramaphosa's inauguration was marked by hope, which was a central theme in his "new dawn" State of the Nation address. Understandably, a country reeling from nine years of organised chaos which resulted in the hollowing out of the state and a sharp decline in growth was expectant that the new era would mark the beginning of economic revival.

However, much of this hope was cautious. This was clear from a decline at the polls in the 2019 national election. Within the ANC, there was an expectation that those loyal to Zuma who were implicated in state capture would be purged from the ANC and government. There were, to be fair, successes, notably the charges brought against ANC secretary general and Free State premier Ace Magashule. But the initial transition from the Zuma era also coincided with profound economic and political turmoil caused by the Covid-19 pandemic and the July riots instigated by members of the RET faction of the party in 2021. The scale of damage to state institutions such as Eskom was also apparent from ongoing looting and incompetence. This marked a new turning point during Ramaphosa's first term: the intensification of rolling blackouts and its impact on businesses and jobs.

Of even greater concern is the perception among all South Africans that the Ramaphosa government has not moved quickly enough, if at all, to halt the economic decline. Disappointment had been turning to anger as households and businesses battling to deal with the interruptions and costs of loadshedding turn their guns on the ANC. Surprisingly, this has not yet been characterised by expected levels of social instability – or anything like the July riots – but there is a pervasive sense that the country is sitting on a time bomb.

More recently, business has come forward, arguing quite publicly that the government has not produced a convincing plan to deal with loadshedding. Their blaming of the president has been accompanied by clamours for parliamentary committees to investigate Ramaphosa's involvement in the Phala Phala saga after the ANC's national conference in December 2022. The party's reputation has not been helped by attempts to block those committees from doing their work and more recent decisions by the government to shield Eskom by exempting the power utility from accounting to parliament in March 2023.

The overall impression created – and this cuts across race and class – is that the Ramaphosa government has built its 2024 election strategy around blocking further exposure of its failings. This strategy, however, is bound to backfire at the polls. A number of factors inform this conclusion.

First, on balance the ANC's chances can be rescued if influential interests and citizens more broadly are given hope that pre-existing legacies of inequality and injustice are being addressed. For if, in retrospect, the promise to turn around these legacies in South Africa has been more aspirational than realistic, tangible outcomes are now urgent. What must be borne in mind is that positive narratives under Ramaphosa are in danger of being lost if the cracks in the foundations of South Africa's democracy deepen. On the current trajectory, things seem to be falling apart, at an accelerating pace.

Second, in different ways, both ideas and institutions can be shields against adversity though only up to a point. Hopeful ideas can evoke positive agency and help mobilise collective action. Institutions can function as shock absorbers. However, both need positive reinforcement, including ongoing attention to festering imbalances. This does not seem to be the case. As Levy has argued, "South Africa's reversal mirrors the ideational turn: an initial season of hope; rising disillusion in the face of continuing (and in some aspect growing) imbalances; and then an ideational shift, an eruption of anger. In the South African case, pressure on institutions came first and the ideational shift came later. Plausibly, in other contexts, a turn to anger could precede, indeed catalyse, a subsequent attack on institutions."

Once a positive trajectory has been lost, what does it take to achieve renewal? As noted earlier, while Ramaphosa began the task of rebuilding the damaged state early in his tenure, he chose an incremental and legalistic path to reform. Ramaphosa did not choose to ignore party bosses and rely on public support for reforms. He relied, instead, largely on hastily repaired prosecutorial authorities to clean up the state. One consequence is that the ANC remains divided, despite

Ramaphosa's victory at the 2022 conference. Resistance remains strong in many regions, cities and towns, and the ANC's hold on majority support in the 2024 election cannot be taken for granted.

Muddling through, without addressing festering imbalances, can fuel disillusionment and cannot continue indefinitely. Ramaphosa has sought to rekindle the aspirations of the 1990s, but more is needed than nostalgia for past promises that may once have offered inspiration but have passed their sell-by date and that are broadly seen by citizens as inadequate to address contemporary challenges.

Third, initiating a new cycle of renewal requires a set of ideas that address the imbalances that have resulted in derailment – including a readiness to challenge incumbent interests that have blocked change. It is imperative that South Africa strengthens the governance and effectiveness of the public sector to stop looting and delivery failures. The country needs to raise revenues to finance a credible commitment to upward mobility and to confront the rigidities that block mobility. It needs to renew a sense of fairness and opportunity. The ANC leadership needs to take the risk of mobilising new coalitions, capable of trumping vested interests that stymie inclusive change. Can South Africa's leadership summon the necessary boldness to rise to this challenge?

Ten

Quo vadis?

In late May 2022, after a two-year lull, my wife and I were thrilled to be back at the Franschhoek Literary Festival (FLF). Shortly after the festival I wrote a column for News24 under the headline "The end of the ANC: Three areas we need to consider".[145] A recurrent theme, I argued, that ran throughout the various interesting book reviews and talks at the FLF was the future of our governing party, the ANC. I recall in particular the "Quo vadis ANC" session facilitated by Adriaan Basson, where Ralph Mathekga and Qaanitah Hunter took turns in dissecting their respective books and the future of the ANC, or the "Thabo Mbeki: A dream deferred" session on Mark Gevisser's book, where the topic of the future of the ANC again came up.

So, in short, we were all talking about books, but there was a looming question about whether the party was over. As I began writing this chapter, in mid-March 2023, the dust that had been kicked up at the 55th national elective conference of the ANC had settled, the new NEC had taken up their leadership roles, a cabinet reshuffle had taken place, and the ANC leadership was in electioneering mode ahead of the 2024 poll. But there was still an undertone of anxiety about the party's prospects in 2024 and beyond. The echo chamber rang with voices amplifying the impending demise of the ANC and celebrating the fact that it would happen sooner than later. Some predicted this would happen as early as the 2024 elections, while others hesitated to say perhaps 2029.

I think we can all agree that the governing party has been losing support. In my previous book, I asked the question: "will Cyril Ramaphosa's ANC survive?" With the 2022 national conference behind us and Ramaphosa firmly in the driving seat of the ANC and government for a second term, the political and economic turmoil gripping South Africa now raises these questions: What are the prospects of the ANC governing South Africa as a majority party? And what are the strategic options ranged before it should it fail to win an outright majority in 2024? Grappling with these questions means understanding, firstly, the pattern of decline over the years and, secondly, the shifting material basis of partisanship, or non-partisanship, over time. I will deal with the party's prospects and strategic options in 2024 in the next chapter.

The contours of growth, 1994–2004

For at least a decade after the first democratic election in 1994, the ANC's liberation ethos had been a key anchor point in its electoral dominance. As a new governing party, its policy choices, accompanied by growth in the formal economy, seemed to correspond to a rise in its support, from 63 per cent of the national vote in 1994 to 66 per cent in the 1999 election.

By the end of the honeymoon period, in 1999, the ANC, led by Thabo Mbeki, remained the country's dominant political party, having defeated its nearest competitor and largest rival at the time, the Democratic Party (DP), by 9,073,993 votes and achieved a further 266 seats in the National Assembly, an increase of 14 seats from those received in the 1994 election. At provincial level, the party swept the electoral board, having won a majority in seven provinces, with only the Western Cape and KwaZulu-Natal (KZN) as exceptions.[146] This trend gained ground between 1999 and 2004, when the ANC's share of votes peaked at 70 per cent.

Within this broad trend, the rising share of the ANC's votes was accompanied by a concentration of the opposition vote behind the newly formed Democratic Alliance, which had emerged from a merger of the DP and fragments of the National Party after the latter's dissolution. However, despite its status as the 'official opposition', having increased its share of the vote from 2 per cent in 1994 to 10 per cent in 1999 and 12 per cent in 2004,[147] the DA had not earned this position by cultivating a broad enough support base that reflected the diversity of South African society, its core support having come mainly from minority groups and urban areas.

I will not deal here with other opposition parties save to say that they, similarly, drew marginal support from either racial or cultural and traditional bases, leading the analyst Bob Mattes to describe voting patterns until that point as a "racial census". Indeed, the apparent stability of voting patterns and lack of electoral volatility had, until 2004, generated consensus among analysts like Mattes that "the composition of partisan coalitions remained largely as they emerged in 1994". The black African population continued to identify with the ANC while minority groups identified with opposition parties.

Moreover, this overall stability is thought to reflect political parties and South African citizens as "'captives' of the historical moment when the new democracy was founded in 1994".[148] The prime bonding agent in the ANC remained political issues surrounding apartheid and its demise, and the party's victory as a liberation movement. Even though structural factors like class, gender, age and geographic inequalities corresponded largely but not exclusively to racial patterns of partisanship, the basis of partisanship was what Collette Schulz-Herzenberg has called "nested cleavages".[149] Partisanship, in her view, reflects "multidimensional cleavage structures in which ethnic categories such as language 'nest' within categories such as race, and are mutually reinforcing".[150]

And so voting patterns reflected the role of liberation – rather than delivery, difference and antagonism – as the fundamental dynamic at work in partisanship. The task assumed by the ANC was to mobilise the active consent of mainly black African voters against the legacy of apartheid rather than focus on delivery as a measure of its electability. But within the ANC and among its allies in the tripartite alliance, debates have raged since 2004 on the fundamental aspects of economic policy and service delivery.

The contours of decline, 2009–2019

The ousting of Thabo Mbeki as party president at the Polokwane conference in 2007 marked the beginning of a period of voter fluidity and decline in the ANC's share of the national vote. Of the three general elections following the historic event of 1994, it was the 2009 election that shifted stable voting patterns and voter preferences. Much was expected after the Polokwane conference a year earlier. Yet that election did not significantly alter the balance of power. The ANC still emerged with an overwhelming majority, except for the Western Cape, where the DA held the balance of power. It also marked the beginning of a period of fierce contestation in local government elections between the ANC and DA.

The impetus for voter fluidity came from several changes in the ANC leadership and a steep, albeit momentary, rise in support for a newcomer, the Congress of the People (COPE). Critics account for Jacob Zuma's election victory as a partial result of the culmination of support for him shown by the ANC Youth League (ANCYL), the South African Communist Party (SACP) and the Congress of South African Trade Unions (Cosatu). Within this new dynamic of fluidity there emerged a lacerating politics of factionalism that cleaved the party between those backing Zuma and Mbeki loyalists; this accounted for the formation of COPE.

Stephen Friedman diagnosed two key issues that emerged from the 2009 election – the role of grassroots voters in electoral politics and the role of identity in voter decisions. The apparent decline in ANC support, in Friedman's view, "challenged the assumption that its new leadership spoke for 'the masses'". In his interpretation of 2009, Friedman wrote:

> That the new ANC leadership was assumed to speak for the grassroots highlighted the degree to which the poor lacked a voice in the national debate ... The 2009 election was about the African National Congress vote – and about two crucial, but often misunderstood, issues in South African politics. For the first time since 1994, the ANC, whose share of the vote had increased in each election, may lose ground. Reports claim that

internal ANC opinion polls have found a loss of support and anecdotal evidence supports this: during a trip to the East Rand after the violence against immigrants from elsewhere in Africa that year, ANC president Jacob Zuma faced vigorous criticism from low-income voters in one of his party's core constituencies, who accused senior politicians of insensitivity to their needs. ANC leaders have acknowledged that it lost ground among voters which it will need to regain during the election campaign. So this was the first election since democracy's advent which was framed in the minds of politicians, voters and analysts as a battle by the ANC to hold onto its base rather than as a campaign to expand its support.[151]

The apparent decline in ANC support challenged one of the myths of contemporary politics – that the victory of Jacob Zuma and his supporters at the 2007 ANC conference in Polokwane was the product of a revolt by "the masses". Zuma and his allies were repeatedly portrayed as the voice of the poor who enjoyed overwhelming support among society's grassroots. In response, Zuma's election signalled a policy turn that would play out at the ANC's 2012 conference as an agenda for radical economic transformation. For the first time since 1994, talk of nationalising the Reserve Bank and land expropriation without compensation emerged in the language of policy debates.

The subtext, however, was far from radical. In reflecting on the RET policy agenda, it is helpful to distinguish between its form and content. While not quite "left-wing", the approach hinged on heavy interventions within an overall context governed by the capture of the state by a political elite led by Zuma. Despite their radical appearance, such policies withered before the left-wing and centrist criticisms they evoked, although much of the opposition around that time was never elaborated into anything coherent.

Whether this was understood by the ANC's grassroots constituency is not clear; what matters is that the ANC's electoral fortunes took a dramatic turn for the worse in the 2014 election. Serious disagreements between the Zuma leadership and the ANC's labour allies had already surfaced at the ANC's policy conference that year, with splits inside Cosatu being an indication of cleavages between the old left and pro-Zuma loyalists.

The ANC won the election but suffered a loss of 3.75 per cent of the overall vote and a deficit of 15 seats in the National Assembly compared to the 2009 election.[152] The official opposition DA increased its share of the vote, winning 1,145,755 votes and 22 seats.[153] There was by then massive impetus towards a new young black voting block around the newly formed Economic Freedom Fighters (EFF). Led by former ANCYL leader Julius Malema, the EFF almost overnight became the third largest party in the country, holding 6.35 per cent of the overall vote and 25 seats.[154]

A drop-off in voter patronage to 62 per cent in 2014, from an increase after 1994 to 66 per cent and 68 per cent under former president Thabo Mbeki, for the first time raised questions about the rootedness of the ANC in the hearts and minds of black South Africans. Much of the drop-off was a result of non-votes. Out of 25.4 million registered voters, 18 million cast their votes, and over 11.4 million voted for the ANC. About 7 million voters chose to stay away. This was something new and demonstrated a turning away from the ANC rather than support for opposition parties.

After the 2009 election, the ANC's support declined sharply, initially in four provinces. Limpopo and Mpumalanga, which recorded the highest number of votes for the ANC in 2009 – at 85 per cent – decreased to 78 per cent. Support in the Free State dropped from 71 per cent to 67 per cent and in North West from 73 per cent to 67 per cent, while support in Gauteng – the country's economic heartland – fell by 11 per cent from 64 per cent to 53 per cent. In the Western Cape, run by the opposition DA, the ANC only managed to increase its support by 1 per cent, to 32 per cent.

Perhaps the dramatic swing was the turn away from the ANC by young urban voters either employed in blue-collar jobs or unemployed. By the time of the local government elections in 2016, several major changes had occurred, particularly in the size of the active ANC electorate. South Africa, as I have argued, had witnessed a general decline in electoral participation in terms of both voter registration and voter turnout. In 2016 the ANC lost many metros in a clear sign that it was taking strain among young urban supporters of the party who, rather than voting for opposition parties, were not voting at all.

Bludgeoned by reputational risk caused by the hollowing out of the state by the RET faction of the party and clamours in parliament by opposition parties for Zuma to pay back money used to upgrade his private homestead at Nkandla, the party's fortunes waxed and waned until Zuma's resignation in February 2018. But the damage was deep. Despite promises by Ramaphosa of policy reform and the removal of corrupt individuals from the party and government, the factionalisation of the ANC and mounting service delivery failures took their toll at the polls in 2019, with the party winning a reduced majority of 57.5 per cent, down from 62.15 per cent in the 2014 election. This was the ANC's lowest share of votes since 1994 and a foretaste, perhaps, of a decline below 50 per cent in 2018.

What are we to make of voting patterns?

Aggregate electoral stability or fluidity can be tested in two ways. The first is the absence or presence of policy change or reforms in the party and their consequences. The second is the underlying stability in the pattern of individual voting behaviour. When aggregate electoral volatility is present, it is often viewed as an indirect indicator of the accumulation of voting shifts.[155] These shifts, as I have argued, are typically evident in either non-voting or a turn to opposition parties. Although the ANC's support base was largely inspired by a desire for services, the failure of state enterprises has hampered service delivery. This suggests that the ANC's dominance, if it will continue to be evaluated against its ability to deliver and its economic performance, is fragile and not long-term. Nevertheless, for the present the ANC's dominance seems assured partly because its support base wants the state to deliver adequately. They hope that it is possible to "catch up materially".

At this point I want to turn to two factors that, I think, will continue to mark the contours of the ANC's decline.

Non-voters

Among non-voters, there are two related considerations that have had implications for the ANC's decline. First, while the eligible voting age population (VAP) had increased by approximately 5 million over the previous decade (due to population growth), the number of registered voters had not kept pace. Between 1999 and 2004 the Independent Electoral Commission (IEC) increased the voters' roll by 2.5 million to 20.6 million voters. Yet, according to VAP figures, the number of votes cast (or overall turnout) actually decreased by roughly 3.9 million from 1994, despite growth in the VAP and in registration.[156]

Second, despite increasing electoral margins for the ANC from 63 per cent to 69 per cent during Mbeki's presidency, the size of the VAP actually voting for the governing party had not increased or even remained static in proportion to population growth. In fact, the ANC's actual support had decreased from 53 per cent to 39 per cent of South Africa's eligible voting population by 2009 when Zuma began his first term.[157] By calculating the proportion of the VAP who voted for the ANC (using total votes for ANC over total VAP), we can see that the ANC had retained 72 per cent of its original 1994 vote share but lost approximately 28 per cent.[158] Significant decreases in turnout and a reduced share of the vote qualify the nature of the ANC's victory in the 2009, 2014 and 2019 national elections, when voter support declined.

Incumbency

I have argued in the previous chapter that much of the country's electoral fluidity has corresponded to abrupt leadership and policy changes since the 2007 policy conference at Polokwane. The consequences of policy reforms have erupted to the surface as the unifying glue of the liberation struggle ethos waned, jobs declined and service delivery faltered under the onslaught of state capture.

This pattern is in stark contrast to the "growth phase" between 1994 and 2004. Since 2009, much of the urban vote seems to be reliant on roughly 18 million people who now benefit from social grants.

Race or incumbency?

In the particular case of South Africa, given that the black support base, which is at the same time a racial or ethnic base, keeps returning the ANC to a position of dominance, is the party's dominance any less legitimate because it is ethnically or racially based? The results from Ipsos, SABC/Markinor, Afrobarometer and HSRC surveys have all suggested that there was stability in voter support patterns for the ANC between the 1994 and 2004 elections. As one might have expected, the ANC's voter support maximised with 69 per cent in the first "liberation" election, a level which has not easily been sustained but which nonetheless remained stable until 2004.

These patterns suggest that bonding had occurred between the ANC and the mass of its electorate, who are black. But scholars such as Bob Mattes have argued that race is no longer the key driver. Instead, ongoing loyalty is driven by incumbency. Of course, incumbency allows dominant parties to sustain these "stable roots in society" and, in the case of the ANC, maintain its rural support base by "indulging in politically calculated disbursements of government funds to rural areas".[159]

Evidence suggests that government spending targeted at urban and rural areas tends to increase during elections, which may to a degree assist the ANC in maintaining its support base. The roughly 18 million people in South Africa reliant on social grants may not all be eligible voters, but the number is large enough to suggest the centrality of incumbency in reproducing patronage. This, of course, is unsustainable. It is by no means a reliable strategy for maintaining voter support. It can be argued that social grants have risen in proportion to the ANC's decline.

Will the party survive?

In a decade of unprecedented drama, a loosening up of party loyalties was bound to happen. The ANC entered democracy as a broad church, dramatically shifted to accommodate new economic realities in the 1990s by abandoning the left, then tried to accommodate all but began losing support among the poor. It did gain the support of the black middle class, who were prime beneficiaries of BEE policies.

The ANC currently holds 249, or 62 per cent, of the 400 seats in the National Assembly, its poorest showing in five successive elections. Furthermore, the ANC's share of the vote dropped below 50 per cent in 2019. Despite this, the ANC's nearest competitor, the DA, still remains far behind, with less than a quarter of the seats in the National Assembly. The actual extent of disarray and decline, though, is potentially more damaging than a few supporters abandoning the party. For the sixth time since the advent of democratic and all-inclusive elections in South Africa, the nation will gather at various polling stations in 2024 to take part in what is regarded as the most contested election in years.

Yet pressing questions remain: Is there an increasing and noticeable race or class basis to ANC support? Are older voters more loyal to the ANC than younger voters? Do rural voters offer greater support than urban voters? And what about other racial groups – is the ANC attracting support outside its traditional constituency after years of democratic government?

There is no reason to expect that the racial composition of the party's support base will change. But within these racial boundaries, especially within the black electorate, I expect there will be some significant changes to the demographic profile of the ANC's partisan coalition since 1994.

The key demographic factors that are expected to have an impact on ANC partisanship are age, class, and urban–rural location. In terms of age, I expect that an older generation strongly correlates with partisanship, reinforcing the notion that ANC support comes mainly from an older black African population. The racial composition of the ANC's partisan coalition is not expected to change significantly since 1994. I also expect to see a reduction in the overall show of support given by minority racial groups. Given their insignificant numbers, I do not expect this to make a difference to the party's performance, however.

Besides increases in non-partisans, or independents, among the black electorate, I expect a new, younger urban cohort of ANC identifiers to drop out of the party's orbit. As younger voters come to dominate the electorate (due to rapid population growth and urbanisation), they will determine the fate of the ANC rather than older ANC identifiers. I therefore expect social and demographic changes to affect the strength of partisanship. Among the younger ANC identifiers, partisanship will be at its weakest in populous urban metros.

In terms of class, I expect signs of growing class differentiation within the black electorate to affect the strength and direction of partisanship as voters start to reward or punish the ANC government for their personal economic gains or losses. Voters who are material beneficiaries of social change, with significant improvements in their education and class mobility, will show greater support and stronger partisan attachments to the ANC government and its basket of social and economic policies, compared with their poorer counterparts. At the same time, those in the black middle class who have benefited from its BEE and employment equity policies will abandon the party if their circumstances change for the worse. It is too soon to make definitive pronouncements, but abandonment of the party by a sizeable number of the black middle class, according to one recent poll, may already have set off alarm bells.

In contrast, I expect the partisan attitudes of the underclass, or those voters deeply affected by poverty and unemployment, to show increasing signs of dissatisfaction with government performance as their expectations of a better material life begin to dissipate. It is probable that the uneven delivery of services, such as energy, water and housing, to communities will begin to affect working-class support for the ANC. I expect urban residents within the underclass to show greater signs of dissatisfaction with the government than their rural counterparts.

It is less certain how black workers will express themselves in partisan terms. Improved employment opportunities for some does not mean improved opportunities for all. While workers in formal employment have generally benefited from rising real wages, there has also been considerable flux in incomes as large numbers of workers lost jobs in recent years.

Two scenarios are likely. My expectations differ depending on the extent to which working-class voters become politicised and develop a class consciousness. As worker perceptions about economic conditions deteriorate, they will become disillusioned with the ANC's centrist economic policy. If this happens, workers who have not enjoyed improvements in their material well-being will lessen their partisan support. On the other hand, other segments of the working class are expected to express their political satisfaction as social spending and economic gains impact positively on employed households who have enjoyed the relative benefits of the ANC's choice of social and economic policies.

Therefore, whereas the ANC's core support was seen in earlier years as the new middle class (the main beneficiaries of post-apartheid redistributive and centrist economic policies), to a lesser extent as blue-collar workers (once the traditional core of ANC support), and least of all as the poorest citizens found within the 'underclass', that dynamic is changing. As the middle class and urban workers abandon the party, its core will shift to the urban underclasses and rural areas. Poorer voters may therefore represent the first source of fluidity within the electorate in 2024.

In terms of the urban–rural divide, I expect that a voter's location in an urban or rural setting will shape the way which they evaluate the government's performance. I think that the urban-based poor, who may have higher expectations in terms of employment and social delivery but have gleaned relatively less in real material improvements since 1994, will begin to withdraw their support for the ANC in 2024. On the other hand, the rural-based poor may perceive greater relative improvements in their quality of life due to social grants, despite high levels of poverty and unemployment. Ironically, the ANC's most vital sources of support may therefore lie with one of the most marginalised sections of the electorate (the rural poor) and their greatest urban beneficiaries (the unemployed), both of which have benefited in a disproportionate manner from incumbency.

What seems clear is the electoral performance of the party corresponds to the economic milestones and policy adjustments discussed in the previous two chapters.

Eleven

2024: What prospects?

When, in November 2022, Cyril Ramaphosa threatened to resign, a huge tremor rippled through South Africa. The event followed a report that found sufficient grounds to consider his impeachment over the Phala Phala scandal. Written by an independent panel appointed by the National Assembly, the report concluded that Ramaphosa may have violated the Constitution and could be guilty of serious misconduct. It seemed a foretaste of the turmoil his departure would cause and the damage it could wreak on the ANC at a time of profound economic and social challenges facing the country. The media jumped onto the story, with dire predictions of the ANC "immediately" losing 20 per cent of voter support if Ramaphosa resigned, according to findings based on one internal poll.[160] The polls generally underscored his popularity, despite the scandal that threatened to derail his political career.

Recognising that the ANC's fortunes in the 2024 election were tied to Ramaphosa, party leaders apparently dissuaded the president from resigning. After all, Ramaphosa had doggedly rebuilt some of the country's institutions and steadily advanced government reform – such as empowering the National Prosecuting Authority, the South African Revenue Service and the Auditor General.

For now, however, the main question on everyone's lips is how far the ANC's support will fall in the 2024 elections and what are the possible scenarios.[161] As the previous chapter has demonstrated, this has become an existential question. In this chapter, I will explore various electoral scenarios in 2024 and their implications for the party and country.

The ground shifts: The 2016 and 2021 local government results

I have argued that the year 2007, when Thabo Mbeki was removed from power in a coup at the ANC's Polokwane conference, was a major inflection point in South African politics. The onset of deep fractures in the party presaged a process of splinters and breakaways from the ANC – by the Congress of the People (COPE) in 2008 and, most consequentially of all, the Economic Freedom Fighters in 2013. It is still early to predict the implications of the fractious nature of the party for its performance in 2024 and beyond. Yet all the signs of terminal decline are there: it has become thoroughly corrupt; it appears unable to reform itself; and it appears increasingly unable to effectively govern the country at national, provincial and municipal level.

For the first time since the end of apartheid, the party's share of votes, nationally, in the 2016 municipal elections dropped below 50 per cent, suggesting that the party's political monopoly was faltering. True, these were only local elections. For now, the ANC continues to govern the country, though its ability to govern municipalities became more tenuous after the 2019 national election. This sharp decline began in 2009, gained ground in 2014 and reached a climax in the 2016 local government elections when support for the ANC fell away dramatically for the first time since 1994. Mired in corruption, the ANC experienced its worst election result in 2016 since taking power, according to media reportage around that time.[162] The *New York Times* commented that widespread anger over a "stagnant economy and the brazen self-enrichment of the ANC's members badly eroded the party's standing, gradually chipping away at its ability to rack up big electoral victories on the basis of its history alone".[163] In what was widely seen as the biggest shake-up of the post-apartheid political order, the party's loss of power in several large metros for the first time suggested that it was losing the urban vote. Countrywide, the party won just over 50 per cent of the vote. "The decline in support", the *New York Times* editorialised, "was especially sharp in eight major cities, where a growing number of black middle-class voters turned against the politics of patronage personified by Zuma and increasingly resisted the ANC's emotive appeals to its heroic past."[164]

Then, in the 2021 local election, the ANC delivered its worst ever electoral performance yet, with support dipping to 46 per cent in local polls nationally. The 2021 election had been widely viewed as a referendum on the ANC, tainted by corruption and facing a backlash over poor stewardship of an ailing economy. For its part, the ANC leadership blamed the poor showing on the Covid-19 pandemic, voter apathy and electricity blackouts imposed by the country's energy utility Eskom.

But as the journalist Stephen Grootes wrote, "in ANC-led councils, there has been more evidence of corruption and the abuse of power (and who can forget a female councillor being dragged out of her office while being assaulted by male security guards in the Amathole District Municipality?)".[165] Grootes went on to say:

> Perhaps the ANC's most public response to its diminution of the voting share was when its head of elections, Fikile Mbalula, blamed the SABC rather than the party's appalling delivery and shambolic management of the campaign. Since then, two instalments of the Zondo Commission's report have been released, laying bare how the ANC allowed, enabled and promoted corruption during the State Capture era. And there is another section (with conclusions) still to come. It is bound to bring more pain.[166]

It did bring more pain. A large number of voters stayed away from the polls, forcing the party into coalitions, which looks like a likely scenario in 2024. In truth, the ANC has been floundering for years. Until 2016, the party had won more than 60 per cent at every election after South Africa's first multiracial vote in 1994 when Nelson Mandela was sworn in as president. The party's support slipped from 62 per cent in the 2011 municipal elections to 54 per cent during the 2016 vote and 46 per cent in 2021.[167]

Chief among the reasons for its failure is the weighty challenge of tackling deep structural injustices bequeathed by apartheid. Inequality, as measured by the Gini coefficient, is now as bad as when black people were deliberately held back by racist laws. Attempts at black empowerment created a small elite, but millions have had to settle for government handouts. Jobs are scarce and schools fail to prepare most children for what few opportunities exist.

Under Jacob Zuma's reign, the bottom simply fell out. His cronies ransacked state coffers and hollowed out institutions; growth slowed to a crawl. While Ramaphosa has tried to reverse the rot, progress is glacial, and thoughts are now turning to the 2024 general election when the ANC may again fail to win outright – this time for the first time in a national election.

And so it was that the first tangible sign of the party's potential loss of its majority in 2024 came shortly after Ramaphosa threatened to resign in December 2022 over the Phala Phala scandal. Poll predictions for 2024 presented in the accompanying piechart were a reaction to Phala Phala. They immediately reduced the ANC's chances in 2024 to 48 per cent of the national vote. The DA appears to have gained, at 22 per cent, with the EFF trailing at 11 per cent of the national share of votes. As a percentage of the total, the opposition party share stands at 52 per cent, nudging the ANC off its perch as the majority party in the National Assembly. Of course, this does not mean that opposition parties will coalesce to gain a majority. In fact, differences between them are far too great for that to happen.

Poll predictions for 2024

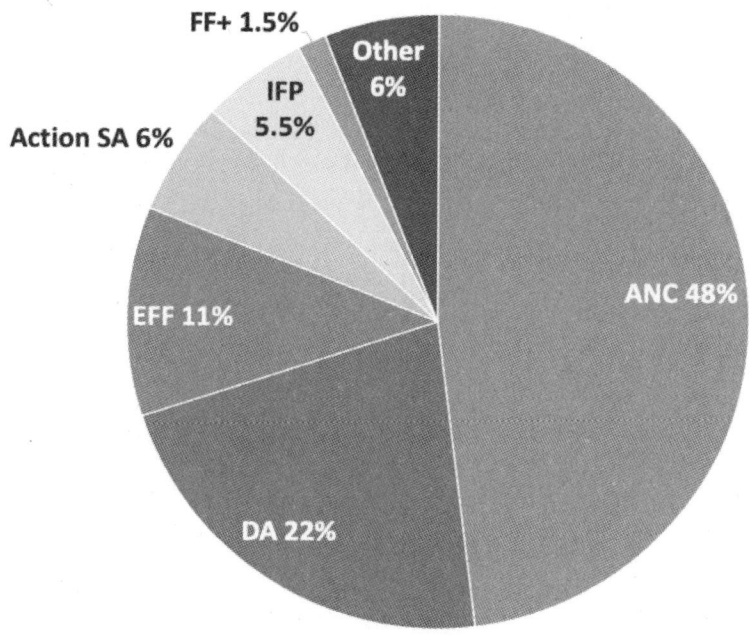

Predictions such as these pose complex questions that were not factored into polling surveys: How bonded are voters to group identity? What class cleavages can be expected to inform partisanship? To what extent is the rural–urban divide a signifier of partisan choices? And to what extent are traditional factors such as the ANC's liberation movement credentials a factor among younger voters?

2024: From partisan loyalties to voter fluidity

South Africa has regressed quite rapidly since 2009, when Zuma became president, so much so that some electoral analysts now argue that traditionally "frozen" cleavage structures and electoral behaviour will change in 2024.

Seeing South Africa through the prism of a highly divided society, some scholars argue that the legacies of colonialism and apartheid still encourage "enduring and inflexible racial and ethnic cleavages" that inform electoral behaviour. The 1994 elections were widely described as a "racial or ethnic census" since the electoral outcome seemed to reflect a link between voter behaviour and race or ethnicity. Three decades later I think that partisan support is more fluid and nested in multiple identifiers, motivated less by group identity. Indeed, there appear to be signs that people's political choices are beginning to be informed by more fluid, cross-cutting interests rather than fixed group identities. The fact of the matter is that South African voters, much like voters elsewhere, now respond to a multitude of short- and long-term factors.

There are several reasons why electoral fluidity will increase among the South African electorate. The first is that partisanship based on race declined after the first decade of democracy because material factors such as service delivery began to replace the liberation ethos that initially carried the ANC to power. Indeed, and this is the second factor, subtle but potentially profound shifts in the motivations of voters appear to have gained ground among ANC supporters. Those shifts were rooted less in the institutional memory of 1994 and more in the performance of the governing party. The third factor is that a rising number of South African voters do not appear to base their partisan stances on primordial racial or ethnic loyalties regardless of political performance. Fourthly, performance evaluations rather than race have played an increasingly more important role over time. Cognitive awareness indirectly affects voter choice by emphasising different types of information but still plays a minimal role in voter behaviour. I believe that they may soon play a larger role in voting behaviour at the polls.

Fifthly, fixed social cleavages hold less sway than ever before. Instead, the indirect influence of race is more complex and feeds into voter decision-making via multiple channels such as government performance and corruption. Voters also appear to look at short-term issues such as retrospective economic evaluations and future economic prospects, as well as party and candidate characteristics such as trustworthiness. In fact, the influence of government performance evaluations on partisanship has grown over the past decade, indicating that partisan choices are increasingly motivated by issues.

In early 2023, polls found that loadshedding topped the list of issues in voters' minds ahead of the 2024 general elections. Polling of registered voters showed the governing party's electoral support slipping below 40 per cent. The results suggested South Africans were so angry with the ANC over power blackouts that they were not considering staying away from the polls as they'd done in previous elections but voting for the DA or EFF in big numbers.[168]

Finally, the fluctuations in partisan alignment and the clear de-alignment trend among ANC supporters should free more voters to move their partisan support to new parties at the polls. However, several of my findings hold negative implications for electoral politics. The first concerns party images. Voters' images of the racialised nature of political parties have shifted somewhat but still remain rigid after close to three decades of democracy. Large numbers of ANC supporters are unlikely to significantly change their partisan allegiances because they see other parties as "exclusive of their interests" or because they are uncertain of whom they represent. In addition, the social environments of many voters generate homogeneous partisan signals that reinforce existing partisan proclivities and perceptions about the racial exclusivity of political parties.

As for the opposition party line-up, most have failed to broaden their appeal among the electorate. Besides opposing the ANC, their policies are weak and ineffective. Together, these factors are bound to minimise partisan fluidity. The chance for a significant realignment is therefore less than some polls predict; although there is greater voter fluidity, electoral predictability, I think, is still rooted in previous voting patterns. While it's possible that the ANC will need partners to remain in government after the 2024 elections, it will probably still have enough support to stave off an opposition coalition government.

But what orientation will emerge in a 2024 government where the ANC is still the largest single party? Will the ANC win a clear majority? If not, will it be DA- or EFF-leaning, or will the ANC be able to cobble together enough smaller parties to get a majority?

Scenarios and outcomes

After the 2021 local elections, several scenarios were sketched, examining what could happen if the ANC fell to 50 per cent or less of the 2024 national vote. So weak has been the ANC's response to the municipal elections drubbing, and so continually lacking were the actions of the government that researchers revised downward some of their predictions ahead of the 2024 poll.

Before the release of the polls, expectations were that ANC support would continue to decline from 57 per cent in 2019 – likely by around 10 percentage points in 2024. Some of the scenarios assumed that the ANC would garner between 38 and 48 per cent of the national vote. This is not a prediction, merely a scenario, but it is not impossible to imagine that the ANC could fall all the way down to 40 per cent.

What, then, are the possible scenarios and strategic options facing the party in 2024? In the section below I explore several scenarios and then draw some conclusions based on my own view of the most likely electoral outcome.

Scenario A: Populist turn
Situation

South Africa is struggling with corruption, poor governance and mismanagement. The ANC – the ruling party since 1994 – is in deep crisis. The lived experience of millions of people in South Africa is likely to become even worse. This is partly due to the government's weak response to the economic and financial crisis, to loadshedding, and what may turn out to be a rising inflationary cycle with deleterious effects on livelihoods. Violent protests may begin. The party leadership comes under pressure to probe Phala Phala in the build-up to 2024. The party's image is plunged into disrepute, forcing Ramaphosa's hand. Ramaphosa steps down and defers to his deputy, Paul Mashatile, to lead the party to 2024. On this path, the dominant ANC faction, led by Mashatile, gains the upper hand but fails to win a clear majority. The ANC enters into a coalition with the EFF, steering a right-of-centre path. As with numerous other national liberation movements in Africa, the ANC increasingly turns to populist policies to retain power.

Pros
- The ANC claims to have done the right thing by probing Phala Phala.

- The party saves face, stumbling along to 2024 with Mashatile as its face, winning just under 50 per cent.

Cons

- Ramaphosa's resignation plunges the country into uncertainty.
- As the ANC is massively divided, the intra-party blame game in the aftermath of such a result would be intense.
- None of that would prevent the party from trying to make a deal with other parties, though, and a showing of 40 per cent would still make it by far the biggest party in parliament.
- Under pressure from the left and RET, Mashatile steers the party towards populism to appease the poor.
- Growth is negative and poverty rises.
- Corruption continues unabated.
- Business confidence plunges to record lows; the rand falls through the cracks; an even greater flood of capital leaves the country.
- The party democratically concedes power but thwarts the popular will by systematically undermining a post-election coalition government, as Zanu-PF did when it entered a coalition with the opposition Movement for Democratic Change (MDC) in 2009, by clinging on to all the key levers of state power.

Scenario B: Stable crisis

Situation

Ramaphosa takes the party to 2024 and scrapes a majority at the polls. In this scenario, the ANC regains some of the urban black vote, including in populous Gauteng, while the DA, ActionSA and EFF struggle. This outcome is likely and will require more decisive leadership than is currently evident. The ANC's election strategy is to reverse the slide into factionalism and downplay corruption by blocking exposure of Eskom while promising to fix the state. At the polls, Ramaphosa wins a mandate, based on hope, to undertake economic reforms needed to fix South Africa over the next five years. This includes fixing Eskom, limiting the size of state-owned entities, ending state capture and expanding public services. Other things that need fixing include reducing red tape to boost entrepreneurship and small businesses, improving the education system, and achieving trade integration in the region. There is a strong emphasis on unity, non-racialism and equality that echoes in Ramaphosa's statements.

Pros

- The party maintains stability in an escalating crisis.
- Many voters cling on to the party as the lesser of all evils while maintaining hope that Ramaphosa's promise to fix the state will eventually materialise.
- With a suitably strong mandate, Ramaphosa undertakes economic reforms to fix the state and reverse the governing party's slide into populism and factionalism.

Cons

- The party becomes complacent and does not see the urgency of reforming fast enough and continues to kick the can down the road.
- Ramaphosa only serves at the behest of the ANC's National Executive Committee. Since the NEC is the principal executive arm of the party, this means that internal ANC factionalism is more important than the electorate.
- Ramaphosa pays lip service to fighting corruption while overseeing a government still rife with it. He pays lip service to good governance while governing South Africa through one of its darkest periods.
- Eskom lurches from crisis to crisis with massive economic consequences.
- Corruption increases or continues on its current trajectory.
- Ramaphosa wants to put the country back on the principled path of non-racialism amid a rising race-based populism. But calling on South Africans to abide by the principle isn't enough. Making this long-standing principle a lived reality, when race still largely defines where South Africans live and work and their life chances, fails to see the light of day.

Scenario C: Centrist coalition

Situation

No clear winner emerges and the ANC enters a coalition with the DA. What the numbers suggest is the possibility of a pact government between the ANC and DA or the EFF and ANC. There is the off-chance the ANC could enter into a coalition with a smaller party like ActionSA to give it a 50 plus one per cent majority. Given the very different ideological orientations of the two larger opposition parties, the ANC's choice under Ramaphosa would be crucial for South Africa's future – basically one between pursuing redistribution or economic growth. There are too many profound differences for a coalition with the EFF. The DA has already publicly labelled the EFF "public enemy number one", cancelling any chance of a coalition between the two dominant minority parties. Ramaphosa positions himself as someone who will reform the ANC and speed up liberalisation and privatisation. He also pledges to clean up the scourge of corruption left behind by the Zuma presidency and set South Africa back on the path of growth. Previously the ANC may have been able to govern in alliance with a batch of smaller parties. But Ramaphosa's growth-first priority chimes with the DA and the latter's earlier statement that it is prepared to join a coalition with the ANC.

Pros

- The growth agenda takes precedence.
- With a clear majority under an ANC–DA coalition, decision-making in parliament is not as chaotic as expected.

Cons

- The ANC loses support among hardened supporters, especially those in the RET faction of the party and its labour allies.
- Decision-making in the party NEC is divided between factions. Paul Mashatile emerges with significantly more support than any other candidate, but with a Top 7 and NEC that continue to reflect stark divisions. The result is a poorly disciplined and uninspiring team with no clear strategy and bad implementation.
- The tripartite alliance fractures and splits, with Cosatu and the

SACP deciding to form an independent labour party, like the MDC in Zimbabwe.
- The ANC enters the 2029 election weaker.

Scenario D: Hung parliament

Situation

No clear winner emerges, and the ANC does not enter into a coalition. A big problem hanging over smaller parties' heads is that they are unable to form a majority coalition. There is chaos after the poll (the ANC is already trying to use this: its deputy president Paul Mashatile recently proclaimed that "there is no party that can replace us"). Decision-making in parliament is difficult, and no clear strategy or policy shift occurs to resolve corruption and the multifaceted crisis in the state. In-fighting in parliament intensifies with the speaker losing control of the House and physical brawls becoming the manner in which disputes are settled. In addition to corruption, governance failure and voter apathy, the ANC's decline in support can be linked to a steady increase in so-called born-free voters and the party's orientation to its rural constituency. To an outsider, the ANC is increasingly a party of self-interest, without a clear vision of its role or South Africa's future. It provides no inspiration.

Pros

- There are no upsides to the scenario.

Cons

- The ANC (like the political landscape generally) continues to fracture.
- Parliament dissolves into messy processes of decision-making.
- A policy vacuum emerges.
- Economic crises and social contestation intensify on the ground.
- Violent revolts spread.
- The economy collapses under the impact of rolling blackouts, business failure and massive divestment.
- Violent crime escalates.
- There is capital flight on a massive scale.

- Those with critical skills and money who can flee to other countries leave.

Results and prospects

What, then, are the likely prospects in 2024? Fresh from his leadership victory after the ANC December 2022 national conference, Ramaphosa cautioned the newly elected NEC that the party would face its toughest challenge yet at the 2024 polls: "In just over a year from now, our country will be holding national and provincial elections. The ANC will probably have to engage in the most difficult election campaign that we have ever fought. The outcome of that election will have profound implications for the National Democratic Revolution and, indeed, for the direction of our country."[169] He had good reason to be guarded. The party has faced dwindling support at the polls in previous national and local elections. The growing energy crisis, high unemployment, corruption, poor service delivery and failing state institutions are believed to be among the reasons South Africans have lost confidence in the governing party.

Ideally, my preference is for the ANC to win a majority so that Ramaphosa has a second chance to deliver on his mandate. In recent months there has been conjecture that if Ramaphosa wins a suitably large majority of the upcoming national vote, he will be able to achieve two notable outcomes. Firstly, he'll be able to reverse the governing ANC's slide into populism and factionalism. Secondly, he'll be able to see off challenges from the EFF, the country's third largest party. He would, in short, have a sufficiently strong mandate to undertake economic reforms needed to fix South Africa.

But critics and opposition party leaders hold a counter-view. They argue that voters vote for the ANC, not for Ramaphosa, and that Ramaphosa only serves at the behest of the ANC's NEC. Since the NEC is the principal executive arm of the party, this means that internal ANC factionalism is more important than the electorate.[170]

Yet the argument is academic if the ANC does not win a clear majority in 2024. Of the scenarios discussed, the real question is whether the ANC will be able to form a durable coalition for a five-year period if it fails to win an outright majority. There is general agreement that the toss-up will be between the ANC entering into a coalition with the DA or EFF as the two dominant opposition parties in the National Assembly and metros or reducing the dominance of these parties by entering into a coalition with one of the lesser parties to tip the scale in the National Assembly.

For its part, the DA has publicly declared its willingness to govern with the ANC. From a policy position, Ramaphosa's market-led growth policy priority is closer to that of the DA than the EFF. But the ANC differs markedly from the DA on foreign policy questions such as relations with Russia and China. My sense is that Ramaphosa's strategic preferences will be dictated by domestic priorities and his growth-first policy stance. In that regard, I think that there is likely to be a stronger lobby from the business community for a kind of "anything but the EFF" solution to a potential coalition.

Many South Africans, certainly in the middle classes and business community, would have sympathy for that arrangement. However troubled it's likely to be, it is, for the middle class, a terrifying option to contemplate a coalition between the EFF and the ANC. As William Saunderson-Meyer has argued, "it really is the worst of all possible worlds" – the EFF is essentially a "stalking horse for the ANC".[171] Many in business and the middle class are pinning their hopes on a 10 to 11 per cent EFF poll and a 35 to 37 per cent poll for the ANC, which would cancel a coalition. But that is unlikely.

What seems clear enough is that coalitions are not a straightforward numbers game; they presuppose deep-seated differences and traditions between the parties. What is equally clear is that the ANC's tactical and strategic choices will be informed by its weakness in the metros where opposition parties have gained ground over the last two local government elections. This pattern of voter patronage belies clear geographic and structural shifts from urban to rural voter patronage for the ANC. If the ANC is to avoid becoming a rural party, it will have to structure its coalition choices on its weakening position in the metros.

Scraping through: My outlook for 2024 and beyond

Now let me express my personal view and preference. I do not think the ANC will fall below the 50 per cent mark in 2024. Contrary to most pre-election polls last year, I think the Social Research Foundation (SRF) survey, based on a sample of 3,204 voters canvassed in July 2022, is a more realistic approximation of the likely result next year.[172] The SRF survey forecasted that 52 per cent of likely voters would choose the ANC if there was a 56 per cent voter turnout at the election, while 50 per cent would vote ANC if the turnout was 66 per cent, even as two-thirds of voters turn to opposition parties and the ANC's support slips further in major cities. The DA would win 25 per cent under both scenarios, the EFF between 11 and 12 per cent, and ActionSA 5 to 6 per cent. The survey had a 1.7 per cent margin of error.[173]

The results contrast with those of several other polls, which showed support for the ANC dipping below 50 per cent for the first time in a national election, as it did in the 2021 municipal vote – a backlash against poor government services and widespread corruption. Ipsos predicted the ANC would win 42 per cent of the 2024 vote, while the Johannesburg-based newspaper *Rapport* said an internal poll conducted by newspaper and other research showed it would garner 38 per cent.

However, the SRF has concluded that "the ANC is wounded but not slain", with its support still concentrated in rural areas and among black voters. The SRF survey goes on to state that the ANC has "surrendered urban South Africa to the opposition", and while "the next decade will likely see South Africa's economic hubs governed by very different political actors to those who control the bulk of its rural heartlands", I think that the ANC, for now, commands sufficient numbers of black voters in urban and rural areas to give it a slight majority nationally.[174]

My preference is that the ANC wins an outright majority. It was Thabo Mbeki's biographer Mark Gevisser who reminded us, at an Franschhoek Literary Festival panel discussion, that it was Mbeki who remarked at some point that if the ANC should fall, it goes without saying that the country will also then fall. In other words, the former statesman was trying to say that South Africa would not survive without the ANC.

Poppycock, I hear most of you saying. After all, author Ralph

Mathekga indicated to the same audience that when the ANC lost power in the three largest metros after the 2016 local government elections, nothing happened. In other words, the country continued to function, so why think that it will not be able to without the ANC. This got me thinking. I would like to highlight a few points which, I believe, centre the discussion on the centrality of the ANC, not only as a majoritarian party but as a hegemonic party.

First, if growth is the top priority facing South Africa, we have to consider that, of all parties, it is the ANC that has steadfastly led a broad coalition of forces since 1994 based on a business-led and business-focused transformation agenda. Despite various changes to the country's macroeconomic and industrial policy framework over the years, the transformation agenda has always presupposed private sector growth as a basic condition for a redistribution agenda. This in turn has presupposed the construction of a sizeable black middle class as a basis for both economic stability and legitimacy. I believe that, despite departures by the Zuma administration from this policy practice, the goals and priorities of the ANC have remained business-centred and market-friendly. In other words, the party has grounded its policies in investment and savings as anchors of the country's monetary and fiscal policies.

However, none of this means that these policy positions are permanent. Much depends on the level of buy-in to a social contract by various stakeholders and sections of society. As things stand, that social contract is tenuous, which explains Ramaphosa's appeal to all parties and stakeholders to join in a national initiative to rebuild the economy. Such buy-in, I contend, will depend on the extent to which a victory by the ANC translates into policies and practices that begin to erode many of the structural and cultural divisions that have fissured South African society.

In a News24 column I argued that anyone who takes a keen interest in South African politics, from colonialism to apartheid to our democratic era, will know that the one phenomenon that has remained overarching throughout our body politic for centuries is racism and racial inequality. And, therefore, any conversation about the future of our beloved country must take cognisance of this very fact. Its resolution is fundamentally a resolution of the structural dynamics of the economic crisis we are in. Any analysis that attempts to deny this reality of racism will fall far short of finding lasting solutions.

And here I want to suggest that the "National Question" (the relationship between historical inequality and race) remains a matter that must be continuously managed. In the same column I argued that attention to the national question started with the Mandela administration; the late president decided to manage the race question at least in part through rugby. Mandela maintained the Bok emblem and opposed fierce fights within his own party over this. The compromises made during the negotiated settlement nowadays go unnoticed and are taken as evident, but it all relates to managing the race question.

During the Mbeki administration, there was more focused attention on the economic basis of racial divisions in the country. Through all this the ANC never abused its parliamentary majority to amend the Constitution on issues such as land. This was another case of managing the race question, in my opinion.

Under Cyril Ramaphosa, as soon as a contingent in the ANC advocated an attack on white monopoly capital and the Reserve Bank, another grouping in the very same ANC made strides to counter such moves. This again was because the race question had to be managed and, in some cases, defended. However, interventions such as these can do no more than manage an untenable set of realities, chiefly very deep structural inequalities that need to be tackled. This means managing expectations between whites and blacks, between labour and business, and between political parties. In this regard, I believe that the ANC is the only political party that has the gravitas and capabilities to manage the entire government and state. Embedded in its culture is the national interest.

The question thus is: do we have a political formation currently that can indeed manage these critical areas? The present alignment of opposition parties poses worrying questions, not least the racial bias of many, with the DA still largely reliant on a white middle-class constituency, the Patriotic Alliance increasingly rallying a coloured constituency, the Inkatha Freedom Party a provincial Zulu constituency, and the EFF a black Africanist constituency.

I am suggesting that we cannot at this stage do without the ANC. Neither can we afford the ANC lapsing into reliance on a black rural constituency as it loses urban support or lapsing into racialised politics in order to garner black votes. And here it is worth quoting at length Roger Southall, who highlights two key features of post-liberation movement rule – such as that by Zanu-PF and the ANC – to help us understand the present crisis in South Africa and the challenges facing the ANC:

> First, liberation movements are characterised by simultaneous democratic and authoritarian impulses. Their claim to having liberated their countries from colonial oppression has much merit. This is true if they are reluctant to share this with other forces which participated in the struggle for freedom. Furthermore, their present claim to be representative of "the people" ensures that they cannot completely ignore the needs of their supporters. On the other hand, they have a long history of authoritarianism. Although they tolerated internal dissent during the freedom struggle, they also quelled it at times with brutal violence. After the arrival of democracy, they have systematically suppressed rivals or allies with a legitimate claim to having contributed to the struggle for liberation. The Zimbabwe African People's Union, led by Zimbabwean liberation struggle hero Joshua Nkomo, was bruised and beaten until it agreed to merge itself into Zanu-PF in 1987. The United Democratic Front, the effective internal wing of the ANC during the latter years of apartheid, dissolved itself following heavy pressure to do so by the ANC in 1991. Both Zanu-PF and the ANC tolerate opposition parties. But they systematically seek to delegitimise them by characterising them as "counter-revolutionary" or agents of foreign powers.
>
> Second, the liberation movements have become the vehicles for rapid class-formation. Although they won political power, they inherited only limited economic power, as the commanding heights of their economies remain in

private hands. Nonetheless, by gaining control over the state, Zanu-PF and the ANC secured control over the state-owned enterprises. In South Africa, these accounted for around 15% of GDP in the early 1990s. Initially, their principal focus was on removing old-guard public servants, whose loyalty to a democratic government could not be assumed, and replacing them with party loyalists who could be trusted. This resulted in the merging of party and state, weakening the independence of bodies of accountability established under their respective constitutions.[175]

And therein lies the heart of the present crisis and challenges. It has been widely acknowledged in polling surveys that South Africa's economic and social imbalances can no longer be swept under the rug. The ANC has three choices: muddle through, endure another surge of ethnopopulism, or pursue inclusive development.

As much as the challenges we face are contemporary, such as the energy crisis and corruption, the heart of the matter is the centrality of the state in mediating a resolution of the national question in a country still reeling from a legacy of structural inequalities. Only the ANC is capable of confronting this legacy. It is, after all, a historical mission set out in the Freedom Charter, the "Ready to Govern" document and the National Development Plan.

Postscript
The unresolved national question

In an article for *The Thinker*, I wrote about the race and class question in post-1994 South Africa and how I think we should tackle it as citizens of this country. It was at the time of Penny Sparrow's and Chris Hart's racist utterances on social media. And since then we have seen yet another racist incident at one of the residences of Stellenbosch University. It resulted in a massive public outcry as did the previous two incidents mentioned above.

What to do about this consistent relic called racism? Pretending there's no white privilege and continuing with our head in the sand just won't cut it any longer. When considering that racism is so prevalent in South African society and wanting to have a correct understanding of the phenomenon, it is essential to look at all three aspects of racism: individual, institutional and structural.

'Colonialism of a Special Type'

The historical injustice of the South African chapter of racism can be found in a very neat theory coined by the ANC–SACP as "Colonialism of a Special Type" (CST). This theory, in short, states correctly that the coloniser and the colonised live side by side within the same borders, which is different from the more typical situation where the coloniser is indeed a foreign power located afar. This is an important theory, and it explains a situation that gave rise to legal segregation of the races, later known as apartheid, which obviously was upheld by fundamental institutionalised racism.

According to Professor Vernellia Randall in a paper titled "Speaking truth to power", institutional racism must be understood as an interaction between prejudice and discrimination. Prejudice, she states, is an attitude that is based on limited information or stereotypes. While prejudice is usually negative, it can also be positive, she contends. No one is entirely free of prejudices, although they may not have any significant prejudice against a particular group. Oppression, she says, is a systemic subjugation of a social group by another social group with access to power. She goes on to say that power is the ability to control access to resources, the ability to influence others, and to control access to decision-makers. Discrimination, on the other hand, is behaviour, intentional or not, which negatively treats a person or group of people based on their racial origins. In the context of racism, power is a necessary precondition for discrimination. Randall further states that racism depends on the ability to give or to withhold social benefits, facilities, services and opportunities from someone who is entitled to them and is denied them on the basis of race, colour or national origin. She concludes that the source of power can be formal or informal, legal or illegal, and is not limited to traditional concepts of power.

Inequalities in power

So, what gave white South Africans this power? Because of the way structural racism normalises white dominance and superiority, it entrenches and perpetuates inequalities in power, access, opportunities and treatment. Because of structural racism, race is not a proxy for disadvantage – it is always and remains a form (if not the only form) of disadvantage.

Professor Pierre de Vos of the University of Cape Town provides us with a solution when he says that one does not address the consequences of structural racism merely by creating opportunities for black people to "assimilate" into the normative white world. Instead, he says, you must transform the society and challenge the basic meaning-giving assumptions according to which society operates and in terms of which goods, services and opportunities are distributed. In short, you attack and dismantle white privilege, which is the flip side of the coin of structural racism.

Institutional racism is not always manifested knowingly and intentionally: its power lies exactly in its ability to make itself invisible. This allows its beneficiaries to deny its existence (and genuinely believe in its absence) while benefiting from it.

The national question

I contend that the current ANC's inability to manage our national question coherently places South Africa at the gravest risk. But let's first backtrack a little. What is "the national question"? The 1997 ANC document entitled "Nation building: The national question in South Africa", outlines the contradictory consequences of colonial conquest in South Africa. On the one hand, colonialism brought together different communities into one nation-state. On the other hand, the colonisers deliberately prevented the unification of the colonised communities into one nation.

The paper explains that "the national question plays itself out in ways that are specific to the concrete conditions in various parts of the world. Nevertheless, it is fundamentally a continuous search for equality by various communities which have historically merged into a single nation-state, or the struggle for self-determination and even secession by communities within such states."

The paper goes on to outline ten theses which should be taken into account in the South African context:
- "Colonialism of a special type" which means that the national character of the National Democratic Revolution (NDR) necessitates the resolution of antagonistic contradictions between the oppressed majority and their oppressors, as well as the resolution of national grievances arising from colonial relations. (This remains an on-going struggle to this day.)
- National oppression and its legacy are linked closely to class

exploitation and so can only be successfully addressed in the context of socio-economic transformation. (Hence the populist politics of attacking white monopoly capital.)
- A nation is not equivalent to a classless society. The NDR requires that all classes and strata – both black and white – act in a way that promotes South Africa's true interests.
- Apartheid was victorious in crippling working-class unity. Reference is made to the Indian and coloured questions as expressions of fear among the working class.
- The national question is also a superstructural phenomenon at the level of consciousness, "feelings" and perceptions. The feeling of pride in being South African cannot be sustained without socio-economic transformation.
- Individuals will have multiple identities, but the main purpose of the NDR is not to promote fractured identities but to encourage the emergence of a common South African identity.
- The main content of the NDR is the liberation of black people in general and black Africans in particular.
- The main content of the NDR should find expression in the leadership structures of the ANC and indeed the country as a whole (commonly referred to "African leadership") but requires that we do "ethnic, racial, language, gender and class arithmetic" in composing leadership structures.
- The national question can never be fully resolved. We must retain a healthy equilibrium between centrifugal (disintegrative) and centripetal (integrative) tendencies.
- The struggle itself was an important and conscious act of nation-building.

Each one of the theses can, of course, be unpicked and elucidated upon, but I won't do that here and now. It must serve as food for thought as we engage in this very critical debate about racism and our part in it. Non-racialism is a by-product of an economically just society. If we can resolve the socio-economic challenges of our country, then the racial challenges will fall away.

Notes

1. Moneyweb 2023.
2. Gevisser 2007, 666.
3. Hirsch 2005, 30–4.
4. Gevisser 2007, 667.
5. Levy et al. 2021.
6. Gevisser 2007, 668.
7. Gevisser 2007, 668.
8. Gevisser 2007, 669.
9. Gevisser 2007, 669.
10. Calland 2006, 125.
11. Calland 2006, 125.
12. Calland 2006, 125.
13. African National Congress n.d.
14. African National Congress n.d.
15. *African Communist* 1997.
16. Calland 2006, 132.
17. Calland 2006, 132.
18. Gevisser 2007, 653–96.
19. Gevisser 2007, 471.
20. Gevisser 2007, 471.
21. Interview, Johannesburg, March 2023.
22. Van Heerden 2017.
23. Maclean 2017.
24. Maclean 2017.
25. Republic of South Africa 2019.
26. Nkosi 2023.
27. The Presidency 2023.
28. Majuqwana 2022.
29. Republic of South Africa 2022.
30. Republic of South Africa 2022.

31 Wood 2022.
32 Sithole 2022.
33 Van Heerden 2022b.
34 Southall 2022b.
35 Southall 2022b.
36 Republic of South Africa 2020.
37 African National Congress 2022.
38 African National Congress 2022.
39 Mavuso 2022.
40 Mavuso 2022.
41 Ray 2008.
42 Hunter and Khumalo 2022.
43 Haffajee 2023.
44 Tandwa 2021.
45 Tandwa 2021.
46 Nicolson 2021.
47 Nicolson 2021.
48 Tandwa 2021.
49 Southall 2022b.
50 Southall 2022b.
51 Southall 2022b.
52 Ray 2009.
53 Ray 2009.
54 Southall 2022b.
55 Southall 2022b.
56 Gevisser 2007, 601.
57 Gevisser 2007, 601.
58 Gevisser 2007, 601.
59 Gevisser 2007, 602.
60 IOL 2022.
61 Tandwa 2022.
62 Tandwa 2022.
63 Mntambo 2022.
64 Koko 2021.
65 Koko 2021.
66 Koko 2021.
67 Koko 2021.
68 Felix and Hunter 2022.
69 Kotze 2012.
70 Nhlabathi *2012*.
71 Hlongwane 2012.

Notes

72 Subramany 2012.
73 Cotterill 2018.
74 Quintal 2017.
75 Ray 2008.
76 Ray 2008.
77 Felix and Hunter 2022.
78 Felix and Hunter 2022.
79 Cowen 2022.
80 Cowen 2022.
81 Detlinger 2022b.
82 Hunter 2022.
83 Hunter 2022.
84 Hunter 2022.
85 Haffajee 2023.
86 Detlinger 2022a.
87 Dubow 2000, 51.
88 Dubow 2000, 51.
89 African National Congress 1992.
90 African National Congress 1992.
91 Marais 1998, 91.
92 See Interim Constitution, Schedule 4: Constitutional Principles of the 1993 Interim Constitution, 244–9.
93 Marais 1998, 92.
94 Marais 1998, 94.
95 Marais 1998, 94.
96 Adelzadeh 2022.
97 Adelzadeh 2022, 148.
98 SA Reserve Bank figures (June 1995), calculated in 1990 constant prices.
99 Marais 1998.
100 Marais 1998, 149.
101 Marais 1998, 192.
102 Marais 1998, 192.
103 Marais 1998, 192.
104 Marais 1998, 192.
105 Gelb 2006.
106 Gelb 2006.
107 Mbeki 1998.
108 Akojee and McGrath 2005.
109 Mthethwa 2011, 32.
110 Mthethwa 2011, 32.
111 Mthethwa 2011, 32.

112 Jeffery 2010, 248.
113 Monyae 2011.
114 Akojee and McGrath 2005, 5.
115 Akojee and McGrath 2005, 5.
116 The Presidency 2009, 2.
117 The Presidency 2009, 4.
118 Mthethwa 2011, 34.
119 Nattrass 2011, 1.
120 National Planning Commission 2012.
121 National Planning Commission 2012.
122 National Planning Commission 2012.
123 Adelzadeh 2022.
124 Adelzadeh 2022.
125 Adelzadeh 2022.
126 Adelzadeh 2022.
127 Adelzadeh 2022.
128 Adelzadeh 2022.
129 Adelzadeh 2022.
130 Adelzadeh 2022.
131 Statistics South Africa 2022, in Adelzadeh 2022.
132 Adelzadeh 2022.
133 Levy et al. 2021.
134 Levy et al. 2021.
135 Levy et al. 2021.
136 Levy et al. 2021.
137 Hirsch 2005, 23.
138 Levy et al. 2021.
139 Levy et al. 2021.
140 Levy et al. 2021.
141 Levy et al. 2021.
142 Levy et al. 2021.
143 Swilling 2017.
144 Levy et al. 2021.
145 Van Heerden 2022a.
146 Piombo and Nijzink 2005, 258.
147 Booysen 2005, 142.
148 Schulz-Herzenberg 2009.
149 Schulz-Herzenberg 2009.
150 Schulz-Herzenberg 2009.
151 Friedman 1999, 12.
152 Mataboge and Letsoalo 2014.

Notes

153 Mataboge and Letsoalo 2014.
154 Mataboge and Letsoalo 2014.
155 Schulz-Herzenberg 2009.
156 Schulz-Herzenberg 2009.
157 Schulz-Herzenberg 2009.
158 Schulz-Herzenberg 2009.
159 Wiseman 1998.
160 Siwele and Cele 2023.
161 Cilliers 2022.
162 Onishi 2016.
163 Onishi 2016.
164 Onishi 2016.
165 Grootes 2022.
166 Grootes 2022.
167 *The Guardian* 2021.
168 Omaree 2023.
169 Mntambo 2023.
170 Mntambo 2023.
171 BizNews 2023.
172 BizNews 2022b.
173 BizNews 2022b.
174 BizNews 2022a.
175 Southall 2022a.

References

Adelzadeh, A. 2022. "Why is the South African economy stuck in chronic crises?". Applied Development Research Solutions Working Paper, May.

African Communist. 1997. "The state and social transformation". First Quarter.

African National Congress. 1992. "Ready to govern: ANC policy guideline for a democratic South Africa". http://www.anc.org.

African National Congress. 2022. *Political Report to the 55th National Conference of the ANC*, December 2022.

African National Congress. n.d. "Discussion document: The organisational design of the ANC's case for internal renewal; An abridged version". http://www.anc.org.za/ancdocs/ngcouncils/2005/org.

Akojee, S. and S. McGrath, S. 2005. "Post-basic education and training and poverty reduction in South Africa: Progress to 2004 and Vision to 2014", *Post-basic Education and Training Working Paper Series*, no. 2, October, Centre for African Studies, University of Edinburgh.

BizNews. 2022a. "ANC likely to win 2024 vote even as city support plunges, survey shows". Bloomberg, 30 August.

BizNews. 2022b. "Polling data shows the ANC a sniff above 50%, Dr Frans Cronje", 2 September.

BizNews. 2023. Interview with Alec Hogg. 14 February.

Booysen, Susan. 2005. "The Democratic Alliance: Progress and pitfalls", in *Electoral Politics in South Africa: Assessing the First Democratic Decade*, eds Jessica Piombo and Lia Nijzink. New York: Palgrave Macmillan.

Calland, R. 2006. *Anatomy of South Africa: Who Holds the Power?* Johannesburg: Zebra Press.

Cilliers, J. 2022. "Amidst debates about presidential impeachment, the main question was how far ANC support would fall in the 2024 elections".

Institute for Security Studies, Johannesburg, 6 December.
Cotterill, J. 2018. "ANC leaders pile pressure on Jacob Zuma to step down". *Financial Times*, 4 February.
Cowen, K. 2022. "Former spy boss Arthur Fraser clams he has evidence that Ramaphosa 'conceals a Crime'". News24, 1 June.
Detlinger, L. 2022a. "Deputy presidency of South Africa is President's call, says party returner, Mashatile". Eyewitness News, 6 February.
Detlinger, L. 2022b. "Section 89 Panel finds evidence of misconduct on 4 charges against Ramaphosa". Eyewitness News, 30 November.
Dubow, S. 2000. *The African National Congress*. Johannesburg: Jonathan Ball Publishers.
Felix, J. and Q. Hunter. 2022. "ANC delegates whipped into line as voting begins". News24, 18 December.
Friedman, S. 1999. "No easy stroll to dominance: Party dominance, opposition and civil society in South Africa", in *The Awkward Embrace*, eds Hermann Giliomee and Charles Simkins. Amsterdam: Harwood.
Gelb, S. "The RDP, GEAR and all that: Reflections ten years later". *Transformation*, 62.
Gevisser, M. 2007. *The Dream Deferred: Thabo Mbeki*. Johannesburg: Jonathan Ball Publishers.
Grootes, S. 2022. "The ANC's 40% in 2024 could bring chaos to an already unsteady democracy". *Daily Maverick*, 13 February.
The Guardian. 2021. "South Africa's ANC on course for worst ever electoral performance in local polls". 2 November.
Haffajee, F. 2023. "Mbeki lashes ANC's block on parliamentary probes into Phala Phala and De Ruyter's Eskom cartel claims". *Daily Maverick*, 30 March.
Hirsch, A. 2005. *Season of Hope: Economic Reform under Mandela and Mbeki*. Pietermaritzburg: University of KwaZulu-Natal Press.
Hlongwane, S. 2012. "Gauteng ANC's first brick in Mashatile's road to Mangaung". *Daily Maverick*, 11 June.
Hunter, Q. 2022. "You are 'constitutional delinquents': Push to oust Mashatile as SG at heated ANC NEC meeting". News24, 10 September.
Hunter, Q. and J. Khumalo. 2022. "Shortlisting, vetting of ANC leadership candidates violates party constitution, special NEC hears". News24, 24 August.
Interim Constitution. 1993. https://omalley.nelsonmandela.org.
IOL. 2022. "David Mabuza's last ditch move to topple Cyril Ramaphosa at ANC conference". 12 December.
Jeffery, A. 2010. *Chasing the Rainbow: South Africa's Move from Mandela to Zuma*. Johannesburg: South African Institute of Race Relations.

References

Koko, K. 2021. "Mabuyane renovated home with portion of R3.3-million Winnie Madikizela-Mandela money". *Mail & Guardian*, 8 October.

Kotze, D. 2012. "The ANC five years after Polokwane". News24, 21 February.

Levy, B., A. Hirsch, V. Naidoo and M. Nxele. 2021. "South Africa: When strong institutions and massive inequalities collide". Carnegie Endowment for International Peace, 18 March.

Maclean, R. 2017. "Zuma impeachment calls grow after court rules on home upgrade scandal". *The Guardian*, 29 December.

Majuqwana, D. 2022. "CR's empty promises brew SA's perfect storm". *Sunday Tribune*, 21 August.

Marais, H. 1998. *South Africa: Limits to Change; The Political Economy of Transition*. Cape Town: University of Cape Town Press.

Mataboge, M. and M. Letsoalo. 2014. "The party's over: ANC sees decline in support". *Mail & Guardian*, 11 May.

Mavuso, S. 2022. "Ace Magashule outside Nasrec, tells delegates 'I am around'". IOL, 16 December.

Mbeki, T. 1998. "Statement at opening of debate in National Assembly on 'Reconciliation and Nation-Building'". Republic of South Africa.

Mntambo, N. 2022. "Sisulu's bid for ANC top 7 suffers final blow". EWN, 18 December.

Mntambo, N. 2023. "Ramaphosa: ANC will face uphill battle in the 2024 election campaign". EWN, 30 January.

Moneyweb. 2023. "All eyes on Godongwana as Eskom debt grows to R422bn". 20 February.

Monyae, D. 2011. "The liberation movement's conception of the pre-1994 South African state". Paper presented at Mapungubwe Institute for Strategic Reflection (MISTRA), Woodmead, Johannesburg.

Mthethwa, R.M. 2011. "New growth path and the transformations of the ANC government policy". *New Agenda, South African Journal of Social and Economic Policy*, no. 43 (Third Quarter).

National Planning Commission. 2011. *National Development Plan 2030: Our Future – Make It Work*. National Planning Commission.

National Planning Commission. 2012. National Development Plan, launch speech by Trevor Manuel, 15 August.

Nattrass, N. 2011. "The new growth path: Game changing vision or cop-out?" School of Economics, University of Cape Town.

Nicolson, G. 2021. "Ace Magashule's R255m case 'bears hallmarks of corruption', says Free State Prosecuting authority". *Daily Maverick*, 12 December.

Nhlabathi, H. 2012. "Gauteng snub of Zuma lays bare leadership divisions". *Sowetan*, 10 October.

Nkosi, N. 2023. "Unplugged". *Sowetan*, 16 January.

Omaree, H. 2023. "Latest polls show ANC has sunk to new lows among voters". *BusinessLive*, January.

Onishi, N. 2016. "ANC suffers major election setback in South Africa". *New York Times*, 5 August.

Piombo, J. and Lia Nijzink. 2005. *Electoral Politics in South Africa: Assessing the First Democratic Decade*. New York: Palgrave Macmillan.

The Presidency. 2009. Green Paper: National Strategic Planning. Pretoria: South Africa.

The Presidency. 2019. "State of the Nation address", February.

The Presidency. 2022. "State of the Nation address", February.

The Presidency. 2023. *From the Desk of the President*. January.

Quintal, G. 2017. "Paul Mashatile gets set to leave Gauteng after being named ANC treasurer-general". *Business Day*, 18 December.

Ray, M. 2008. "Mr President?". *Finweek*, 17 January.

Ray, M. 2009. "Zumanomics: Dancing to everybody's tune … for now". *Finweek*, 9 April.

Republic of South Africa. 2020. "Address by President Ramaphosa to a Joint Sitting of Parliament on South Africa's economic reconstruction and recovery plan", 15 October.

Schulz-Herzenberg, C. 2009. "Towards a silent revolution? South African voters during the years of democracy 1994–2006". PhD thesis, University of Cape Town.

Sithole, S. 2022. "Ramaphosa is a spy, working with the CIA – Zuma". IOL, 21 November.

Siwele, K. and S. Cele. 2023. "Ramaphosa's resignation would cost ruling party a fifth of votes". Bloomberg, 6 January.

Southall, R. 2022a. "South Africa is in a state of drift: The danger is that the ANC turns the way of Zimbabwe's Zanu-PF". *The Conversation*, February.

Southall, R. 2022b. "What is RET and what does it want? The Radical Economic Transformation faction in South Africa explained". *The Conversation*, 7 December.

Sowetan. 2012. "Gauteng snub of Zuma lays bare leadership divisions", 10 October.

Subramany, D. 2012. "Mangaung: The ANC's newly elected Top Six". *Mail & Guardian*, 18 December.

Swilling, M. (convenor). 2017. *Betrayal of the Promise: How South Africa Is Being Stolen*. State Capacity Research Project, Cape Town, May.

Tandwa, L. 2021. "The ANC's step aside rule explained: past, present and what's next for Ace & co.". *Mail & Guardian*, 2 May.

Tandwa, L. 2022. "David Mabuza nags Zuma for backing". *Mail & Guardian*, 7 October.

References

Van Heerden, O. 2017. "Cyril, Gordhan et al. and their Gordian knot," *Daily Maverick*, 24 April.

Van Heerden, O. 2022a. "The end of the ANC: Three areas we need to consider". News24, 21 May.

Van Heerden, O. 2022b. "A case of wag the dog? Fraser will have to prove his claims". News24, 9 June.

Wiseman, J.A. 1998. "The slow evolution of the party system in Botswana". *Journal of Asian and African Studies*, January.

Wood, W. 2022. "SA at risk of investor isolation amid a perfect storm of financial markets". *Business Maverick*, 2 December.

Index

2010 Soccer World Cup 19–20

A

Accelerated and Shared Growth Initiative of South Africa (ASGISA) 118–119, 125
ActionSA 167, 169, 173
Adelzadeh, Asghar 124
African Transformation Movement (ATM) 96
Afrobarometer 155
Akoojee, Salim 119
Alex Mafia 99
Amathole District Municipality 161
ANC Veterans League 47
ANC Youth League 16, 19, 81, 85, 135, 140, 150
Auditor General 159

B

Bailey, Quintin xvi
Basson, Adriaan 147
BEE Commission 45, 139
Bernstein, Rusty 109
Betrayal of the Promise 141
Black Economic Empowerment (BEE) 45, 71, 123, 139, 141, 156, 157

Blackhead Consulting 64, 65
Botha, P.W. xv

C

Calland, Richard 9, 12
Cambridge 19
Cape Flats xvi
Cape Town 2–3, 20, 98, 101, 180
Cape Youth Congress (CAYCO) xvii
Cedar Secondary School xvii
Child Support Grant 138
China 2, 116, 172
Cholota, Moroadi 65
Chris Hani Memorandum 86
Colonialism of a Special Type (CST) 179, 181
Communist Party 8, 19, 132
Congress of South African Students (COSAS) xviii
Congress of South African Trade Unions (Cosatu) 11–12, 14–16, 60, 71, 85, 150, 152, 169
Congress of the People (COPE) 19, 135, 140, 150, 160
Constantia xvii
Constitutional Court 29, 88, 133
Convention for a Democratic South

Africa (Codesa) 73
Covid-19 xi, 1, 32, 33, 35, 53, 63, 64, 70, 97, 125, 126, 131, 143, 161
CR17 77
Craighall 20
Creamer, Kenneth 14, 22, 49
Cronin, Jeremy 9, 13
Crown Mines 15, 48
Cuba 15, 65

D
Daily Maverick xix, 25, 26, 27, 28, 70
Davos 34
De Klerk, F.W. 13, 132
De Vos, Pierre 180
Defiance Campaign 110
Democratic Alliance (DA) 148, 149, 152, 156, 165, 167, 169, 172, 173, 175
Democratic Party (DP) 148–149
Department of Correctional Services 95
Diamond Hill 65
Digital Vibes 70, 73
Diko, Khusela 63–64
Diko, Madzikane II Thandisizwe 63–64
Dlamini-Zuma, Nkosazana xi, 27, 28, 69, 72, 76, 77, 92
Duarte, Jessie 23, 46, 80
Dubow, Saul 109–110
Durban 11, 74

E
Eastern Cape 54, 66, 81, 84, 102
Economic Freedom Fighters (EFF) 86, 152, 162, 165, 166, 167, 169, 171–172, 173, 176
Economic Reconstruction and Recovery Plan 33, 46
Energy Action Plan 33, 35
Engels, Friedrich 16
England 19
Eskom xii, 33–36, 131, 143, 144, 161, 168

F
Finweek 89
Franschhoek Literary Festival (FLF) 147, 173
Fraser, Arthur 38, 96, 97, 98
Free State 21, 64, 65, 77, 143, 152
Free State Department of Human Settlements 64–65
Freedom Charter 8, 9, 109–110, 111, 115, 177
From the Desk of the President 34

G
Gauteng 77, 84, 85, 87, 88, 152, 167
Gauteng Department of Health 64
Gauteng High Court 97
Gevisser, Mark 8–9, 11, 12, 74, 147, 173
Gigaba, Malusi 78
Gordhan, Pravin 28
Grootes, Stephen 161
GroundUp 25
Growth, Development and Redistribution (GEAR) 12, 15, 65, 71, 115, 116, 117, 118, 119, 124, 125, 134, 137, 140
Gupta brothers 23, 65, 78

H
Hanekom, Derek 3, 101, 102
Hani, Chris 13, 86, 132
Hart, Chris 179
Harvester Primary xvi
Hirsch, Alan 8, 130, 137, 138
Hunter, Qaanitah 147

I
Independent Electoral Commission (IEC) 154
Independent Newspapers 25, 27
Inkatha Freedom Party (IFP) 21, 175
Interim Constitution 111

Index

International Monetary Fund (IMF) 8–9, 114
Ipsos 155, 173

J
Joemat-Pettersson, Tina 92
Johannesburg Stock Exchange 3
Jordan, Pallo 86–87

K
Kimberley 2, 101
Kotze, Dirk 85
KwaZulu-Natal (KZN) 52, 69, 72, 73, 76, 148

L
Lamola, Ronald 79–82, 83–84, 90–91
Lekota, Patrick 16, 18, 19, 135
Lenin, Vladimir 9, 16
Levy, Braun 8
Levy, Brian 135, 136, 137, 141, 142, 144
Limpopo 37, 77, 152
London Stock Exchange 139
Lungisa, Andile 54–55, 65–68, 78
Luthuli House 7, 18, 43, 46, 47

M
Mabe, Pule 92
Mabuyane, Oscar 79–82, 83–84, 90–91, 102
Mabuza, David 54, 76–78, 80, 82, 84, 88, 100, 101, 104
Macroeconomic Research Group (MERG) 113–114
Madikizela-Mandela, Winnie 81
Madonsela, Thuli 141
Mafikeng 7, 9–15, 41
Magashule, Ace 20, 23, 54, 57–58, 64–66, 68, 70, 76, 77, 81, 99, 143
Magwenya, Vincent 98
Makhura, David 14, 49, 88
Malema, Julius 85, 135, 152

Manana, Naph 14
Mandela, Nelson xviii, 7, 8, 14, 15, 31, 71, 74, 84, 104, 129, 131, 132, 136, 162, 175
Mangaung 18, 20–22, 72
Mantashe, Gwede 92, 101–103
Manuel, Trevor 1, 9, 32
Mapisa-Nqakula, Nosiviwe 96–97
Marais, Hein 111–112, 115, 117
Marx, Karl 16
Masekela, Hugh 31
Mashatile, Paul 50, 80, 82, 83–92, 95–105, 166–167, 169, 170
Masondo, David 92
Mathabatha, Stanley 92
Mathekga, Ralph 147, 174
Mather, Tahera 70
Mattes, Bob 149, 153
Mbeki, Thabo xiv, 8–17, 19, 20, 23, 27, 31, 35, 42, 43, 45, 52, 53, 59, 63, 70–72, 73, 74, 84, 85, 86, 89, 104, 115, 116, 118, 129, 131, 134, 139, 140, 147, 148, 150, 152, 154, 160, 173, 175
Mboweni, Tito 22
McGrath, Simon 119
Memory and Forgetting 109
Minorco 139
Mitchell's Plain xvi, xvii
Mitchell's Plain Action Committee xvii
Mitchell's Plain Student Congress (MIPSCO) xvii
Mitha, Naadhira 70
Mjongile, Songezo 21
Mkhize, Zweli xii, 42, 52–53, 62, 69–70, 72–73, 74, 76, 77, 83–84, 88–91, 92, 102, 103
Mkhwebane, Busisiwe 81
Mokoena, Refiloe 65
Mokonyane, Nomvula 92

Moodley, Spongy 7, 47, 48
Morogoro 74, 86–87
Moscow 8, 9
Mostert, Walleen xvii
Motlanthe, Kgalema 10–11, 18, 20–21, 52, 54–55, 60–63, 65–68, 88, 140
Movement for Democratic Change (MDC) 167
Mpambani, Ignatius 65
Mpumalanga 21, 84, 102, 152
M-TAG Systems 65

N

Nasrec Expo Centre xi, 22–23, 25, 27, 28, 30, 36, 39, 40, 41, 42, 47, 57, 58, 70, 77, 88, 126
National Assembly 29, 88, 96, 148, 152, 156, 159, 162, 172
National Democratic Revolution (NDR) 181–182
National Development Plan 177
National Development Plan Vision 2030 121
National Executive Committee (NEC) xiv, 3, 9, 11, 13, 17, 39, 54, 57, 58, 60–61, 62–66, 68, 69, 74, 75, 76, 85–88, 92, 99–100, 101, 147, 168, 169, 171
National General Council (NGC) 120
National Party 13, 73, 111, 113, 149
National Planning Commission (NPC) 120–121
National Prosecuting Authority (NPA) 65, 89
National Treasury 85, 122, 124
National Union of Mineworkers (NUM) 73
Nattrass, Nicoli 114
Ndlovu, Mandla 102
Netshitenzhe, Joel 14, 22
New Growth Path (NGP) 120
New York Times 160–161

News24 xix, 38, 100, 147, 174
Nkandla 23, 29, 85, 87, 88, 135, 141, 153
Nkoana-Mashabane, Maite 88
Nkomo, Joshua 176

O

Office of the Secretary General (ANC) 44

P

Paarl xvii
Pakenham, Thomas 90
Pan Africanist Congress (PAC) 19
Patriotic Alliance 175
Phala Phala xii, 3, 37–39, 96–104, 143, 159, 162, 166
Phosa, Mathews 85
Pollsmoor prison xvii
Polokwane 16–19, 21, 29, 43, 59–60, 69, 71, 84–85, 89, 134, 140, 150, 151, 154, 160
Polokwane SACP–Cosatu–ANC Youth League alliance 85
Port Nolloth 3
Potgieter, Febe 14, 49, 92
Premier League 20, 23, 77
Presidential House 3
Prevention and Combating of Corrupt Activities Act 81
Prevention of Organised Crime Act 81

R

Radebe, Jeff 9, 14
Radical Economic Transformation (RET) 16, 17, 20–23, 26, 27, 28–29, 30, 32, 37, 40, 41–44, 45, 46, 51, 52, 53, 54, 58, 59, 61, 62, 64, 65, 66–68, 70–73, 75–79, 82, 89, 90, 92–93, 98, 100, 143, 151, 169
Ramaphosa, Cyril xi–xix, 1–14, 22, 23,

25–40, 41–45, 52–54, 58, 59, 60, 61, 62, 63–64, 67, 69–75, 76–82, 83–84, 88–93, 95–106, 123, 126, 127, 131, 143–145, 148, 153, 159, 162, 166, 1770, 171–172, 174, 175
Ramokgopa, Gwen 50, 92, 99
Ramokgopa, Maropene 92
Randall, Vernellia 180
Rapport 173
Ray, Malcolm 15, 89
Ready to Govern 110, 113, 115, 124, 177
Reconstruction and Development Programme (RDP) 8, 9, 12, 14, 71–72, 113–117, 135–138
Regional Executive Committee 61
Release Mandela Committee 73
Reserve Bank 18, 22, 29, 38, 112, 140, 151, 175
Robben Island 87
Rocklands xvi
Rosebank 48, 96
Russia 58, 172

S
SABC/Markinor 155, 161
Sachs, Michael 14, 48, 49
SADC 97
Saul, Zamani 2–4, 101–103
Saunderson-Meyer, William 172
Saxon 99–101, 103–105
Schulz-Herzenberg, Collette 149
Season of Hope 8, 1347
Secretary General's Office (SGO) 44, 74
Serote, Wally 17
Sexwale, Tokyo 85
Sisulu, Albertina 78
Sisulu, Lindiwe 69, 78
Sisulu, Walter 78
Skweyiya, Zola 86
Slovo, Joe 13

Sobukwe, Robert 19
Social Research Foundation (SRF) 173
Solidarity Fund 35
South Africa Inc. xiv
South African Communist Party (SACP) 8, 9, 11, 12, 13, 14, 15–16, 71, 85, 150, 170, 179
South African Revenue Service (SARS) 38
Southall, Roger 42, 71, 72, 176
Sowetan 34
Sparg, Marion 29
Sparrow, Penny 179
Special Branch xvii
Special Investigating Unit (SIU) 42
Speed, Steyn 14, 25–27, 82
State of Capture 141
State of the Nation Address (Sona) 35, 45
State Security Agency (SSA) 95
Stellenbosch University 179
Strategy and Tactics 9
Student Representative Council (SRC) xvii
Sunday Independent 63
Survé, Iqbal 27

T
Tambo, Oliver 74, 86
Thinker, The 179
Through the Eye of the Needle 60
Top 7 xix, 74–75, 79, 91, 169
Truth and Reconciliation Commission (TRC) 133
Tutu, Desmond 133
Two Minutes to Midnight xi, xix

U
Umkhonto we Sizwe (MK) xvii
Union Buildings 18, 104
United Democratic Front (UDF) xv, xvi, xvii, xviii, 99

United Nations (UN) 133
University of Cape Town (UCT) 180
University of Durban-Westville 74
University of the Witwatersrand 42

V
Vavi, Zwelinzima 85
Veale, Gloria xvii
Victor Verster prison xvii
Vlok, Adriaan xvii

W
Waterberg xii, 37
West Wing 16, 104
Western Cape Student Congress (WECSCO) xvii
World Economic Forum (WEF) 34
World Health Organization (WHO) 133

Y
Yengeni, Tony 55, 66
Yeoville 20

Z
Zanu-PF 167, 176–177
Zikalala, Snuki 47
Zimbabwe African People's Union 176
Zondo Commission of Enquiry in State Capture 30, 72, 96, 161
Zondo, Raymond 30
Zuma, Jacob xi, 1, 12, 16–23, 25–30, 32, 33, 37, 38, 43, 45, 52–53, 55, 58, 69, 70–73, 76–77, 84–89, 96–97, 103, 120, 122, 126, 131, 134, 135, 139–143, 150–153, 154, 161, 162, 163, 169, 174